MW01221798

Along the Grapevine Trail

Stanley Talbott

VINEYARDS AND WINERIES IN
SOUTH DAKOTA, WYOMING, & NEBRASKA

BY STARLEY TALBOTT

South Dakota State Historical Society Press ⟶ Pierre

Along the Grapevine Trail

© 2008 by the South Dakota State Historical Society Press
All rights reserved. This book or portions thereof in any form
whatsoever may not be reproduced without the expressed
written approval of the South Dakota State Historical Society Press,
900 Governors Drive, Pierre, S.Dak. 57501.

Library of Congress Cataloging-in-Publication data
Talbott, Starley.
Along the grapevine trail : vineyards and wineries in
South Dakota, Wyoming, and Nebraska / by Starley Talbott.
     p. cm.
Includes bibliographical references and index.
ISBN 978-0-9777955-7-4
1. Wineries—United States—South Dakota. 2. Wineries—
United States—Wyoming. 3. Wineries—United States—
Nebraska. I. Title.
TP557.T35 2008
641.2'209783—dc22
                    2008008501

The paper in this book meets the guidelines for permanence
and durability of the Committee on Production Guidelines for
Book Longevity of the Council on Library Resources.

Design by Rich Hendel
Please visit our web site at www.sdshspress.com.

Printed in China

12 11 10 09 08   1 2 3 4 5

FRONTISPIECE
Vitis riparia is a hardy grape that grows wild across the
United States. Breeders crossed it with domestic varieties
to create vines that will thrive in the harsh climate of the
Northern Great Plains. *Courtesy David J. Ode*

For Beauford,
who shares my love of
a great adventure

CONTENTS

ACKNOWLEDGMENTS

With sincere gratitude I thank many people for making this book a reality. It all started in 2004, when three former schoolmates, Beauford Thompson, Carol Eckhardt, and I sat sipping milk shakes at the Chugwater Soda Fountain after a high-school reunion. Carol and Beauford had recently moved back to farms in the area, and Carol mentioned that she was thinking about planting grapes on her small acreage. Beauford thought he would like to try that, too, and I thought they were both a little crazy. Beauford and I had been high school sweethearts, had parted upon graduation, married others, and raised families. Then, both single, we began dating again after the school reunion. In spring 2006, shortly before Beauford and I were married, we planted a small vineyard. I learned that almost no one knew that grapes could be grown in Wyoming, so I began writing a book about vineyards and wineries on the high plains of the West, including South Dakota and Nebraska.

My thanks go to Bruce and Patrick Zimmerer, who first allayed my fears about planting grapes in a harsh climate and told me the fascinating story of their vineyard in southeastern Wyoming. From there I traveled the highways of three states to meet the many pioneers of this new enterprise. I thank all those wonderful people in Nebraska, South Dakota, and Wyoming who opened their doors to me and told me about their experiences. I hope I have done them justice in telling their stories.

I thank my husband, Beauford, for his patience on each journey and for his chauffeuring duties. He also served as my first reader and gentle critic, for which I am grateful.

My appreciation goes to Olga Crespin of San Antonio, Texas, for babysitting our vineyard and cats while we made some of our grapevine tours. She also put her careful eye to the manuscript and made helpful suggestions.

Thanks go to Nancy Tystad Koupal, director of the South Dakota State Historical Society Press, for believing in my idea and ultimately publishing *Along the Grapevine Trail.*

I am most grateful of all for Patti Edman, associate editor of the South Dakota State Historical Society Press. Patti was able to take my manuscript, nurture it with care, and prune it, producing a vintage crop.

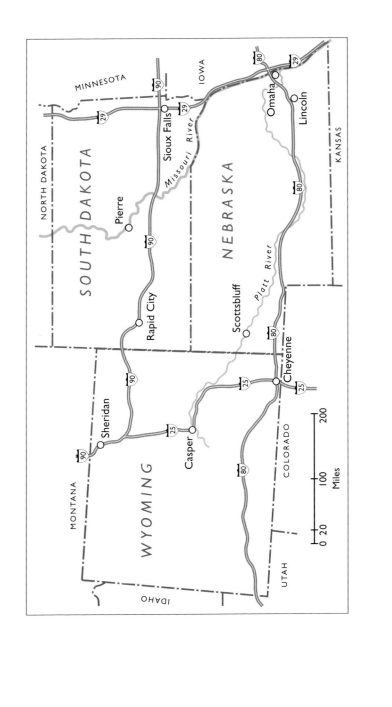

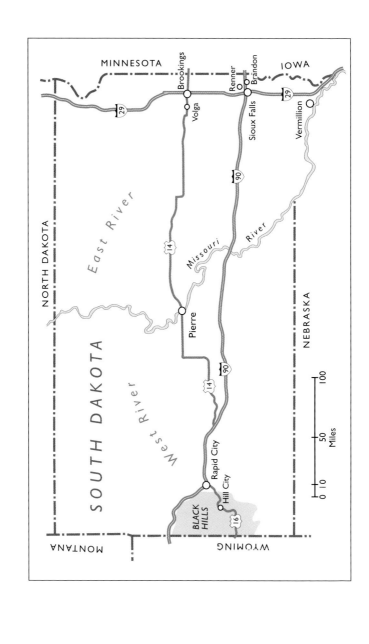

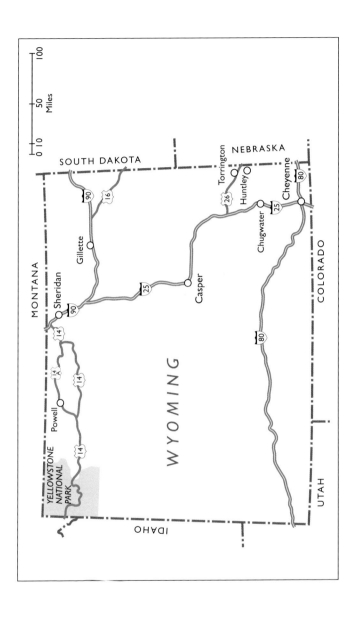

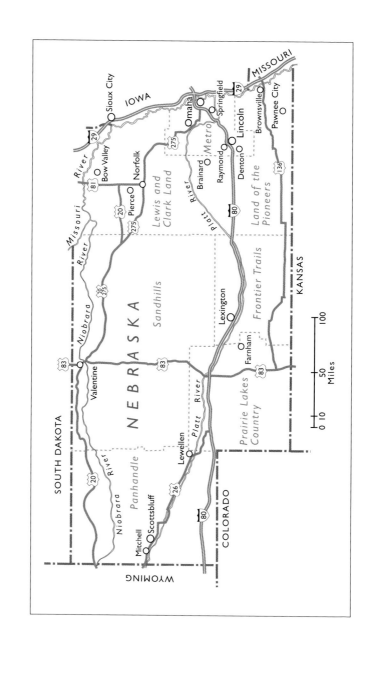

Along the Grapevine Trail

INTRODUCTION

The wind is the only constant. It flows over the Rocky Mountains onto the eastern prairies, sometimes with the force of a thousand stampeding bison, sometimes like a whisper on a moonlit night. Once the wind whistled only through the prairie grasses, but then the homesteaders came, and the wind tossed the crops they planted. Farming on the prairies was always a challenge, but research from agricultural universities helped farmers adapt and contribute to the breadbasket of America. As time went on, small acreages and new agricultural ventures grew up alongside large ranches and farms. Established growers began looking for alternative crops. In the past, it was unthinkable to plant commercial vineyards on the windy plateaus and alternately frozen and sun-baked prairies of the Northern Great Plains. Today, hardy vines are yielding grapes that produce interesting new wines.

The long history of wine is interwoven with the culture of mankind. No one knows for certain who produced the first wine, but it is thought to have originated in the Mediterranean region thousands of years ago. Wine may have been one of the first things man created by accident; grapes have concentrated sugars and ample juice that allow them to ferment on their own. Playing an important role in religion and social exchange since ancient times, wine has been used as a medicinal substance and as an accompaniment for food. Ongoing research and controversy surround potential health benefits, but moderate wine use continues to enhance human enjoyment of food and social interaction. As festivals and events grow up along the grapevine trail in the Northern Great Plains, wineries and vineyards contribute new excitement to the culture of the region.

On the northern plains, interest in grapes began soon after the settlers arrived. Nebraska growers developed a grape and wine industry in the late 1800s and early 1900s, putting five thousand acres into production. Following World War I and Prohibition, however, most Nebraska vineyards went out of business. Nearly six decades later, in the mid-1980s, commercial grape production resumed. South Dakota and Wyoming, with their cooler climates, did not develop wine industries until more cold-hardy varieties of grapes became available. The University of Minnesota pioneered the development of these grapes through a state-funded research program led by Elmer Swenson, a dairy farmer from Wisconsin who started work at the university in 1972. He and other researchers developed cross-bred grapevines with names like Swenson Red, Frontenac, Saint Croix, LaCrescent, and Marquette. Swenson crossed wild *Vitis riparia* grapes with French hybrid vines and, in conjunction with the university, released the Swenson Red and LaCrosse varieties in 1978. *Vitis riparia*, also known as riverbank grape, is a hardy and vigorous wild grape that grows successfully from Canada to Texas and from Arkansas, Tennessee, and Virginia west to the Rocky Mountains. This particular species is useful as rootstock because it is resistant to the soil-borne pest phylloxera and can withstand the cold winters of the Northern Great Plains.

The most popular cold-weather variety was introduced in 1996. The Frontenac grape reflects the best characteristics of its parents, *Vitis riparia* and French hybrid Landot. Frontenac vines are hardy to thirty-three degrees below zero Fahrenheit, are disease resistant, and produce heavy, small black grapes in medium to large clusters. Introduced in 2002 and combining *Vitis riparia* and Saint Pepin, the white grape variety LaCrescent produces a vine that is cold hardy but not as disease resistant as others. In 2003, the white Frontenac Gris also promised to be a good variety for cold-climate grape growers. In 2006, Marquette, a grape derived from Frontenac and Pinot Noir, became an exciting new addition to the grapevines grown in cold climates. Elmer Swenson died in 2004 at the age of ninety-one, but his legacy lives on for grape growers in cold-climate states. Ed Swanson, who established Cuthills Vineyard, Nebraska's first farm winery, near Pierce, Nebraska, in 1994, follows in the footsteps of Elmer Swenson and researches grape breeding. Swanson is considered by many to be the grandfather of Nebraska's current vineyard and wine industry.

The concept of a farm winery began in 1976, when New York State passed the first legislation allowing farmers to produce and sell wines. The Nebraska Farm Wineries Act passed the state legislature in 1986, and South Dakota passed similar legislation a decade later in 1996. The definition of farm winery varies from state to state. In Nebraska, a farm winery need not be located on a farm, but it must use at least seventy-five percent Nebraska-grown produce in its wine. In South Dakota, the 2008 legislature voted to remove language allowing only farm owners to operate a farm winery. The state now defines farm winery as any winery producing wine with a majority of ingredients grown or produced in the state. Nebraska allows farm wineries to produce no more than fifty thousand gallons of wine a year, and the wineries may sell their product either onsite or through retailers or wholesalers. South Dakota increased the production limit to one hundred fifty thousand gallons in 2008. Each state also offers some tax incentives. All farm wineries must be licensed, although an operation can be licensed but not yet producing enough wine to sell. Farm wineries are considered by many states to be a way to encourage consumption of locally grown products and to provide economic support to the agricultural sector through tourism and alternative crops. Farm winery legislation has been introduced in Wyoming, but as of 2007, it had not passed the state legislature. That state defines a winery as a "commercial enterprise manufacturing wine at a single location." There is no reference to the source of the ingredients.

In 1994, the same year that Ed Swanson established his vineyard, the University of Nebraska began an extensive research program to help growers become established. By 2006, Nebraska wineries produced forty-nine thousand gallons of wine and had a direct economic impact in the state of $2.4 million, according to the Bureau of Business Research at the university. The state had twenty licensed farm wineries in 2006, plus twenty-six vineyards that grew grapes but did not produce wine. The Nebraska Winery and Grape Growers Association, a nonprofit organization that promotes the grape and wine industry and provides information for member grape growers and winemakers, has divided the state into seven different zones, each with different soils and climate, that enable vintners to produce wines with characteristics unique to a particular location. Nebraska wineries included in this book are grouped within these zones.

South Dakota State University has also been instrumental in developing grapes that thrive in the harsh conditions of the Northern Great Plains. Retired professor Ronald Peterson began developing a hardy grape in the late 1950s, one that could withstand both heat and cold as well as wide temperature fluctuations. He walked along the Missouri River bottoms in Montana looking for wild grapes that could be crossed with domestic varieties to produce a vine that would grow under stress. Luckily, Peterson found the wild *Vitis riparia* before they died out completely as a result of farm chemicals and changes caused by the Missouri River dams. Peterson crossed the wild grape with Fredonia, a hardy New York State variety, creating the grape he named Valiant. Released in 1983, it proved to be one of the hardiest grapevines grown anywhere. Eldon and Sherry Nygaard of Vermillion, South Dakota, named their business Valiant Vineyard as a tribute to the Valiant grape. They became the first commercial winemakers in the state, planting their initial vines in 1993. The Nygaards were also instrumental in passing legislation in 1996 that allowed farmers in the state to make and sell wine. By 2007, South Dakota State University reported fourteen licensed farm wineries in the state, although not all are actively bottling wine. South Dakota is divided roughly in half by the Missouri River, and residents refer to the regions as East River and West River. The wineries discussed in this book are divided into these regions.

The University of Wyoming established a grape-testing plot

at its Sheridan Research and Extension Center in 1987, proving that grapes could be grown on the cold and windy plains of Wyoming. Prior to 2001, there were only two wineries in Wyoming, making wine mostly from grapes purchased from other states. One of those wineries has since closed. The Zimmerer family of southeastern Wyoming established the first large-scale vineyard and winery in 2001. Patrick Zimmerer helped change restrictive liquor laws in Wyoming in 2006, enabling Wyoming wineries to sell directly to consumers and retail outlets.

This book offers a sampling of the vineyards and wineries in these three states, offering a cross section of old and new, large and small vineyards. Location, innovative growing methods, and ability to host visitors contribute to whether or not a vineyard is featured. A more comprehensive list of vineyards in the three states occurs as an appendix. Except where noted, photographs are the product of my camera. Beginning with South Dakota's oldest winery, Valiant Vineyards in Vermillion, those who wish to follow the grapevine trail can visit the other East River wineries, then travel along Interstate 90 to Prairie Berry Winery in the Black Hills. A drive south through eastern Wyoming would take the traveler to that state's only winery, Table Mountain Vineyards in Huntley, along with the vineyards in the area. Those willing to take a more extended trip could visit Rocky Ridge Vineyard in northwestern Wyoming before heading south along United States Highway 26 to Prairie Vine Vineyard in Mitchell, Nebraska. Interstate 80 east will then take the traveler to many of the vineyards and wineries in Nebraska. A side trip to northern Nebraska would allow tourists to visit Cuthills Vineyard, the state's oldest winery, along with others featured in this book. The grapevine trail would then end back where it began at Valiant Vineyards.

Nebraska, South Dakota, and Wyoming vintners are actively working to provide opportunities for people to visit vineyards and wineries within their states. They are establishing trails, planning festivals, and developing brochures and Internet sites. The person who follows the grapevine trail can learn about the history of winemaking, the growing of grapes, and the making of wine. Each winery provides travelers with the opportunity to taste different varieties and explore regional variations. Special events geared to different seasons invite visitors to return to experience grape crushing, multicourse meals, or harvest rituals. The information contained in this book is current as of the date of publication. Hours and activities at vineyards and wineries are subject to change, however, and many operations accept visitors only by appointment. Travelers are advised to call or e-mail the vineyard or winery in advance of a visit. This book offers armchair travelers and motorists alike the opportunity to pursue their own grapevine trail and sample the new flavors of the ancient culture of wine, now transplanted to the Northern Great Plains.

South Dakota

Co-owner Sherry Nygaard greets visitors to
Valiant Vineyards near Vermillion, South Dakota.

EAST RIVER
Valiant Vineyards Vermillion, South Dakota

The pioneer settlers who homesteaded Turkey Ridge Creek in the 1880s passed on their courage to descendant Eldon Nygaard, who, along with his wife Sherry, established a vineyard and winery more than a century after his forebears first farmed the fields of eastern South Dakota. Eldon and Sherry Nygaard named their new enterprise Valiant Vineyards, in part as a tribute to the cold-hardy Valiant grape developed by South Dakota State University. It also took valor to start the first licensed winery in South Dakota.

Once their first planting of Valiant vines produced a crop, the Nygaards wanted to establish a winery, but the state had no enabling legislation. Undeterred, they authored a farm winery bill that became law in 1996, allowing South Dakota farm wineries to make up to fifty thousand gallons of wine annually and including tax-based incentives for using South Dakota-grown products. The bill, Eldon Nygaard said, was "meant to diversify the economy, create jobs, and use some land that's not usable for anything else." The odds were against them, Sherry Nygaard added. "People told us we couldn't grow grapes in South Dakota and we couldn't market wine in South Dakota. . . . It was a valiant effort that has paid off very nicely."

A South Dakota native, Eldon Nygaard was an army helicopter pilot in Vietnam and earned two Distinguished Flying Crosses and a Purple Heart. After graduating from the University of Nebraska at Omaha and obtaining a law degree from Marquette University, Nygaard taught business and political science at Arizona State University, Colorado University, Marquette University, and the University of South Dakota. He currently serves on the board of directors of Wine America, a nonprofit trade association. Originally from California, Sherry Nygaard worked as a flight attendant and in the hospitality field in Nevada. She graduated from the University of South

Grapes are pressed into juice at Valiant Vineyards. *Courtesy of Valiant Vineyards*

Dakota in 1997 and worked at a computer company before leaving to handle special events at Valiant Vineyards and manage the winery's private restaurant.

The couple moved to South Dakota in 1993, buying a farm near Viborg where Eldon had grown up. "I was a city girl," Sherry said, "but we'd come to visit relatives in South Dakota often and always had fun with the farm activities. We both decided we wanted to live in South Dakota and try farming." The couple planted mostly row crops but also two acres of grapes, including several varieties of French hybrids such as Saint Croix, Frontenac, Seyval, LaCrosse, and Kay Gray in addition to the Valiant grapes. The Nygaards joined the Minnesota Grape Growers Association and received advice from professors at South Dakota State University. "Many people bent over backwards to help us get established," Sherry Nygaard said. They eventually moved the winery to the bluffs overlooking the confluence of the Vermillion and Missouri rivers at Vermillion, next to the Buffalo Run Resort Bed and Breakfast.

In addition to the grapes from their own vineyard, the Nygaards also purchased grapes from other growers throughout the region. "We wanted to spread the risk around. Chances are that all the vineyards in the area wouldn't have a loss at the same time, and we'd at least get fruit from someone," Sherry Nygaard said. In making their wine, the Nygaards also import grape juice from California. "By law, seventy-five percent of the juice has to come from the named wine," she said. "We add South Dakota fruit juices to these wines to make our own stamp. We've been able to get our wines shelved in nearly every liquor store in South Dakota because we have wines named Merlot and Chardonnay." Retailers will put such wines next to California wines, allowing Valiant Vineyards "to compete in the wine and tourism market."

Each year, Valiant Vineyards produces a wine to commemorate the Sturgis Motorcycle Rally. *Courtesy of Valiant Vineyards*

Eldon Nygaard is the winemaker at Valiant Vineyards winery, which has twenty-two brands sold in five European countries and throughout South Dakota. The winery's signature wine is its Wild Grape, made from South Dakota's native grape, *Vitis riparia*, growing wild on his property. This wine, which *Wine Spectator* called "most unusual," sells at a wine shop in Paris for one hundred dollars a bottle. Wild Grape has been mentioned in *Time* magazine, *New York Times*, *Wine Spectator*, *USA Today*, and *Farm Journal*. "Our wines are crafted in the passionate tradition of old-world winemakers," according to Eldon Nygaard. He creates wine using such winemaking techniques as malolactic fer-

During harvest, visitors can stomp grapes the old-fashioned way. *Courtesy of Valiant Vineyards*

mentation (introducing bacteria that changes malic acid to lactic acid, softening the taste), barrel aging, and cellaring to bring forth the natural character of the fruit. "I'm most proud of our Wild Grape wine that has become world famous. It's really a great experience to create and taste its unique flavor," he said.

In keeping with the pioneer spirit that led them to establish Valiant Vineyards, the Nygaards named their first white wine Courage (a semidry wine from a blend of Kay Gray, La Crosse, and Seyval grapes) and their first red wine Northern Valor. They have also established their wines as part of a well-known tourist event, the Sturgis Motorcycle Rally. Held each August, the rally attracts hundreds of thousands of riders from all over the world. The Nygaards produce wine each year with a special label commemorating the event. Sturgis 2005 is a dark maroon-colored wine, similar to cabernet sauvignon, with flavors of oak and fruit. It is described as "soft and very well-mannered with the advantage of being rich and supple but only moderately tannic." Sturgis 2006 is a merlot. Some of Valiant Vineyards other popular wines include Turkey Ridge Creek Chardonnay, a dry white wine with flavors of ripe fruit and oak, and Pasque, a blush wine named for the South Dakota state flower.

Visitors to Valiant Vineyards have many choices, including daily wine tastings and tours of the winery, South Dakota-made items in the gift shop, banquet and meeting rooms for large and small groups, and a bed and breakfast. The bed and breakfast has five themed rooms, such as the Queen Anne room and the frontier room, containing king- or queen-size beds, private bathrooms, and Jacuzzi tubs. Each Labor Day weekend, Valiant

Vineyards hosts the Great Dakota Wine Fest, which brings vintners and tourists from all over South Dakota to celebrate one of the state's newest agricultural enterprises. From their one-hundred-thirty oak-barrel room, three-thousand-gallon fermentation tanks, and fifteen-hundred-bottle-an-hour production line to the comfortable tasting room with a buffalo-themed mural and cozy fireplace, the Nygaards make it clear that you do not have to be in California to produce and enjoy fine wine.

Bird netting covers the mature grapes before harvest at Dakota Falls Winery in Brandon. *Courtesy of Dave Howard*

Dakota Falls Winery Brandon, South Dakota

Big and bold describes the wines and the winemaker at Dakota Falls Winery. With a hearty handshake and a big smile, Dave Howard welcomes visitors on Splitrock Boulevard in Brandon, just south of Interstate 90. Dave, his wife, Mary, and their children are the backbone of the family operation. The vineyard with twenty-five hundred vines is located three miles east of Brandon in the Sioux River Valley.

"As grape growers, we believe that only by tending our own vines can we produce the highest quality grapes and finest wines we want our customers to enjoy," said Dave. "In addition to growing vines for our winery, we are testing fifteen different varieties of grapes for South Dakota State University and the University of Minnesota." The Howards started their vineyard in 1997 and, like other growers in the area, planted cold-hardy grapes including Valiant, Frontenac, Marechal Foch, Leon Millot, De Chaunac, Seyval Blanc, Kay Gray, LaCrosse, Elvira, and Edelweiss. In creating his wine, Howard uses only South Dakota grown grapes, adds no other fruits, and does not age his wine in oak barrels.

Howard grew up in central South Dakota and attended college at South Dakota State University in Brookings. He served twenty years in the army as a commissioned officer. After living away from the state for many years, he moved home and found himself immersed in a second career in winemaking. "I enjoy the business, I love making wine, and I get great joy in producing a quality product," he said. Howard took an extension course in winemaking from the University of California at Davis before he became a winemaker. He opens the winery in Brandon by appointment and is otherwise at the vineyard, where he and his family do most of the work. Unlike growers in drier parts of the region, producers in eastern South Dakota do not irrigate their vineyards because the area averages twenty-three inches

Plump grapes await harvest at Dakota Falls Winery.
Courtesy of Dave Howard

of rainfall a year. Howard's vineyard management practices include using a one-wire trellis system, leaving sod between the rows, using a little nitrogen, and putting a netting canopy over the vines to keep out the birds. Howard often hires youth groups during harvest time to pick grapes as fund-raisers.

Owner Dave Howard pours wine and welcomes visitors to his winery.

Often on the road promoting his wine and the South Dakota wine business in general, the Howards "take our product out and promote wine tastings all over the state," he said. "It's fun. You gotta have fun. Life's too short if you don't have fun." Because of these activities and the growing wine culture in the region, "more and more people are finding out about South Dakota wines," Howard reports with a smile, "and they feel comfortable trying them out. We like people to ask questions. There are no rules of wine tasting. Sure, people think they have to swirl the wine in the glass and smell it and gaze at it, but, hey, I tell them to just try it and don't worry about the rules."

Dakota Falls Winery's labels include: Splitrock Red, a medium-bodied red wine blended from Frontenac and Valiant grapes; Ringneck Red, a bold red wine blended from Marechal Foch and Frontenac grapes; and Harvest Gold, a white wine blended from Seyval and Kay Gray grapes. These and other wines are available at the winery in Brandon and at wine shops throughout the state. Scheduled bus tours visit Dakota Falls Winery, and the Howards participate with nearby wineries in group tours, including the Garden and Winery Tour in May and the Tannenbaum Trail Winery Tour in December. Everything at Dakota Falls Winery is one-hundred-percent South Dakota made—big and bold.

Wilde Prairie Winery Brandon, South Dakota

Visitors to Wilde Prairie Winery can enjoy fine wines while reminiscing about what life might have been like for the former occupants of what was known as Chase Farm. The farm's century-old two-story farmhouse is home to the present owners, Jeff and Victoria Wilde, and their children. The farm is located just west of Splitrock Creek on "wonderful rolling hills perfect for growing grapes," Jeff Wilde said. The family moved there from California in 1991, raised a few head of cattle, planted a few grapes, and became hobby winemakers. "Friends kept asking us if they could buy some of our wine," Victoria said. "So we started looking into getting licensed." They became South Dakota's ninth farm winery in July 2004.

The Wildes started out with thirty-five Valiant vines and now have thirteen hundred vines, including Frontenac, Marechal Foch, Seyval Blanc, LaCrescent, and Valiant, along with fruit trees and bushes. "We produce many fun wines, among them our dandelion wine," Victoria Wilde said. She is the winemaker, and Jeff is the vineyard manager. Friends and family help in harvesting, "especially the dandelions," Jeff Wilde said. "We sit at the picnic table and pluck the yellow petals until we can't stand it any longer," he added with a laugh. They currently produce about twenty gallons of dandelion wine each year to fill approximately one hundred bottles.

Victoria Wilde had taken a college class on viticulture in California. She also joined the Minnesota Grape Growers Association and found it helpful to attend workshops. Because the first grapevines the Wildes planted were Valiant vines, the cold-hardy grape developed at South Dakota State University, Victoria Wilde enjoys making wine from those grapes. "Even though some vintners don't think Valiant makes a very good wine, I love working with it. It's very different and has the most beautiful purple color when made into wine. I don't blend it with other grapes. I like to make straight Valiant wine," she said. Along with the Valiant grape wine they call Prairie Red, the most popular wine at Wilde Prairie Winery is Dandelion Wine. Their other wines include American Frontenac, a semidry red; Rhubarb Wine, from fruit grown on the farm; Apple Wine, a fall favorite from local trees; and Mead, a wine fermented from South Dakota honey with flavors of alfalfa, clover, and oak.

Victoria Wilde pours wine at Wilde Prairie Winery near Brandon

Both Jeff and Victoria Wilde have other jobs—Jeff is an engineer and Victoria teaches fitness classes. They spend at least one hour and up to five hours a day on their farm chores, especially tending vines and making wine. Victoria is also an artist and painted the tree that adorns their wine labels. "It was a beautiful tree at the back of the property that I photographed and then decided to paint. It looks wild and winsome and somehow defined how we feel about our winery," she said.

Picnics and potluck dinners, accompanied by wine tastings, are often featured at Wilde Prairie Winery. Along with fellow local winemakers, the Wildes host the Tannebaum Trail Winery Tour in December and the Garden and Wine Tour in May. Guests spend the day visiting six destinations on a chartered bus. The tour includes wine tasting, garden tours, lunch, and shopping. The tour leaves from the Center for Active Generations on Forty-Sixth Street in Sioux Falls and travels to Belly Acres Greenhouse in Baltic, Dakota Falls Winery in Brandon, Oak Ridge Nursery and Landscaping in Brandon, Prairie Petals Nursery in Brandon, Strawbale Winery in Renner, and Wilde Prairie Winery in Brandon. Lunch includes a wine tasting hosted by Schadé Vineyards of Volga.

The Wilde's property includes a former dairy barn with a hip roof that at one time was home to dozens of dairy cattle. Inside, slivers of blue sky and golden sun peak through rafters, cast-

This barn is the future winery and tasting room of Wilde Prairie Winery.

Victoria Wilde's painting of an old tree on the property became the background for the winery's labels. *Courtesy of Victoria Wilde*

ing shadows across the empty wooden floor. The Wildes hope to transform the barn into their winery and tasting room in the years to come. Out on the prairie where dandelions bloom, the cows graze, and the grapevines meander, visitors can wander into a historic barn and taste the fruits of the vine. If they show up on the right day, the guests just might find themselves plucking a few dandelion blossoms.

Strawbale Winery Renner, South Dakota

Strawbale Winery is tucked between a one-hundred-year-old barn and a grove of trees. The building appears to be a simple house or small barn, but the name hints that this winery is unusual. Don and Susie South constructed the winery of compacted straw and straw bales. The unique material provides a controlled environment for the wine cellar. "Our straw building has the ability to re-create the controlled environment of cellars and caves that have always played an important part in the maturation of great wines," Susie South said.

Opened on 1 November 2006, the unique building has been inspected by hundreds of visitors. The outside and inside walls of the tasting room are stucco, and the windows have eighteen-inch-wide window wells. Inside, the Souths left two "windows" open into the straw-bale insulation where visitors can see how the building was constructed. The tasting room, with a cathedral ceiling and wide wood floors, is finished with yellow pine from Minnesota. Old-fashioned wooden pegs hold the beams and boards together. The only metal is in the steel roof. The walls of the winery have an insulation factor of R-45 and the ceiling is R-50. "The remarkable insulating properties of straw bale has meant we are able to reduce the energy needs of the winery as well as use a product that would have otherwise gone to waste," Don South said. "This building marries our commitment to environmental sustainability and production of fine wine."

The tasting room has a playful feel. Don and Susie South invite guests to sit on high stools at a counter made of chalkboard slate reclaimed from a local school that was closed. Customers can taste wine and write their favorite wine names on the chalkboard counter as they taste Grandpa Pete's Strawberry Rhubarb Wine, made from Don's Grandpa Peterson's rhubarb; and Jalapeno, a white wine flavored with a kick of hot pepper.

Trees surround the winery and tasting room at Strawbale Winery near Renner. *Courtesy of Strawbale Winery*

Family and friends helped place the straw bales during construction of their winery. *Courtesy of Strawbale Winery*

The bestsellers at Strawbale Winery are Grandpa Pete's Strawberry Rhubarb Wine and Black Currant Wine. The couple's favorite is "whatever we just bottled," said Susie South.

The couple "landed in South Dakota ten years ago," Don South said. They had taken a trip to New Zealand and stopped at a winery. The owner had written a book about cold-weather variety grapes; they tasted wines and bought the book. "As they say, 'the rest is history,'" he said. The Souths have planted a one-acre vineyard near the winery. A six-acre vineyard is located a two-hour drive away, where Don and Susie often go to work with their Frontenac, LaCrosse, Frontenac Gris, LaCrescent, and Saint Pepin vines. Both husband and wife are wine masters. Like many other vintners, they started producing wine as a hobby using a winemaking kit and progressed to more sophisticated methods. For fermenting, they now use plastic vats and a three-hundred-gallon refrigerated

Susie and Don South invite visitors to taste their wine and view the unique construction of Strawbale Winery.

steel tank that was converted from a dairy tank. They use a half-ton bladder press for extracting the juice and sometimes blend wines with fruits they purchase from local growers. They use no oak barrels but sometimes add oak or jalapeno chips during aging. Most of their wines are aged from six months to two years. Don South's seventy-six-year-old father, Bob, helps out at bottling time. "He does a great job bottling, corking, and labeling each bottle, one at a time," Don South said.

The Souths host meetings, bridal showers, wedding rehearsals, and family reunions. "One of my favorite groups is the Red Hat Ladies that sometimes meet at the winery," Susie South said. "The organization includes several older ladies that seem to really have a blast when they come here." The Souths also collaborate with other vintners to host the Tannebaum Trail Winery Tour in December and the Garden and Winery Tour in May. Strawbale Winery, with its prairie-style buildings, vineyard, and animals reminds visitors of country-style living. It is also an example of environmentally friendly construction and sustainable methods of operating a vineyard and winery.

Schadé Vineyards Volga, South Dakota

Earth, water, sun, and time combine to form the elements that define the wines at Schadé Vineyards. Jim and Nancy Schade emphasize the homegrown quality and people-friendly environment at their vineyard and winery in eastern South Dakota. "People find it unbelievable that you can grow grapes in South Dakota," Nancy Schade said. "We want to share our story with our guests, and we want to learn their stories." The friendly atmosphere is evident in the tasting room, where children can play with toys and drink hot chocolate while adults enjoy a glass of wine. "Europeans have a much healthier approach to dealing with alcohol. Wine is served with meals there, and children learn from an early age that alcohol consumed in moderation is a good and healthy thing to do," Nancy Schade said.

The Schades moved to their farm west of Volga in 1999 and planted two acres of grapes consisting of Valiant, Frontenac, and Kay Gray vines. Each year they added other varieties of grapes and planted fruit trees such as chokecherry and native buffalo berry bushes. Their winery was licensed and opened in 2000. "It was a hobby that got out of hand after a friend gave us a winemaking kit," Jim Schade said. The couple furthered their interest after touring the vineyards of Napa Valley, California. Their wines blend homegrown produce with fruit from twelve other producers in the area.

The Schades enjoy being involved in a new industry. "We are people who are dreamers and risk-takers," Nancy Schade said. "We find it very fulfilling to work with other people who embrace those qualities and are new in the wine industry, too." She described the vineyard business in South Dakota as "value-added agriculture and economic development." The Schades have been involved from the beginning in "growing" the new industry. They are working to establish a South Dakota Wine Growers Association and to change state laws that do not per-

Standing next to a row of Valiant grapevines, Jim Schade discusses vine varieties during a field day at Schadé Vineyards near Volga. *Courtesy of Schadé Vineyards*

mit South Dakota producers to ship their wine directly to individuals within the state, though they can ship wine to certain other states. When the Schades began their new venture, they both worked full-time away from the farm—Jim as an estate planner and Nancy as academic coordinator for students with disabilities at South Dakota State University in Brookings. "One day, Jim said one of us would need to quit our full-time job in order to keep the vineyard and winery growing. I got my hand in the air first," Nancy Schade said.

Jim Schade is the master winemaker, and Nancy is the marketing manager. She said her staff is "pretty much me, myself, and I." They hire college students to help out in the winery, especially with bottling. They often hire students with disabilities. "It takes a little more time, and we write everything down step-by-step for a disabled student, but it's also helped the rest of us and added to quality control because now everyone uses the list we developed for the disabled students," she said. The students have fun working in the winery and add humor and vitality to the organization. "There is one young woman who works at bottling who likes to sing. One day she was singing away in the winery. I was hosting a small group in the tasting room above. . . . When she finished her song the guests upstairs applauded. It added to everyone's enjoyment of the day," Nancy Schade said.

Harvesting is a special time at the vineyard. Friends pitch in, along with the hired help. "The entire year's work is brought

Jim Schade explains vineyard management practices to a visitor.
Courtesy of Schadé Vineyards

together at harvest time," Jim Schade said. "You have to find just the right sugar content in the grapes and be ready to harvest before the birds get there first." Workers pick the grapes by hand, place them in wagons, and haul them to the press on the back porch of the winery. The juice of the pressed grapes is mixed with juices from other locally grown fruits and transferred to plastic fermenting vats. "Time takes over and magic takes place," Jim Schade said. "You can see, smell, and hear the

Nancy Schade dispenses wine and conversation in the tasting room of Schadé Vineyards.

flavors and bouquets that are unique to our area during fermentation."

When the time and wine are right, bottling begins. "Soil, wind, water, and the fresh air of South Dakota are the elements that provide the quality and homegrown taste of Schadé Vineyard wine," Jim Schade said. They produced five hundred cases of wine in 2000, and, six years later, they bottled three thousand cases of wine. The winery specializes in blended wines with a fruity flavor, including rhubarb, plum, chokecherry, raspberry-apple, strawberry-rhubarb, Kay Gray, mead, and their signature wine, Oakwood Red, a blended blush wine made primarily from Valiant grapes. "When we worked with the Valiant grape, we found it worked best to blend it with another fruit to temper its 'foxy' finish," Nancy Schade said. They like to work with the Valiant grape in spite of its sharp bite because it was developed at South Dakota State University and fits in with their overall plan to use South Dakota products. "We're also very fond of the Kay Gray grape that makes a nice, sweet white wine," said Jim Schade. Elmer Swenson, the Wisconsin dairy farmer who helped develop the first cold-hardy grapes in conjunction with the University of Minnesota, developed the Kay Gray grapes.

Visitors to Schadé Vineyards in September are invited to

participate in a harvest festival that includes food, music, and a grape stomp. "If they participate in the grape stomp, they can have a wine made from the juice they produce. We'll make a holiday wine for them with a specialty label," Nancy Schade said. Schadé Vineyards also hosts a customer appreciation day in November, a holiday open house in December, an evening of wine and roses for Valentines Day, and a family Easter egg hunt. Three words describe what Jim and Nancy Schade want visitors to find at their winery: experience, taste, and enjoyment. "We are here to listen to our customers," Nancy Schade added. "I recently had a friend come to buy wine for a celebration before sending her son off to fight in the war in Iraq. She poured out her heart and sadness to me as we sat and sipped a glass of wine. After that she was able to go home and be strong for her family and her son before sending him off to war." Homegrown fruit and hospitality are the ingredients for a satisfying experience at Schadé Vineyards.

Prairie Berry Winery Hill City, South Dakota

In the Black Hills of South Dakota, artist Sandi Vojta is at work. Her palette is a silver tank, her watercolors range from a delicate pink strawberry to the deep purple of a wild choke-cherry. The finished work resides in a bottle that may be stored in a cellar for years or immediately poured into a glass and enjoyed. Vojta has been a commercial winemaker since 1998, but her training started years earlier. As a toddler, she gathered wild berries with her father, Ralph Vojta, and helped him make wine from her great-great grandmother's wild berry recipe. "It's in my blood to be a winemaker. It's who I am," Sandi Vojta says. She has a degree in chemistry and biology but considers the artistry most important in making wine. "During the fermenta-tion of the fruit, I feel, I see, I taste. The wine becomes me and I become the wine," she said.

Prairie Berry Winery began in Mobridge, South Dakota, in 1998, moved shortly thereafter to Rapid City, and then in 2004 relocated to its current home in Hill City. But the winery's roots were sown deep in the Dakota soil near Mound City in 1876, when Vojta's great-great grandmother, Anna Pesa Vojta, first made wine from the "prairie berries" she found growing nearby. She and her husband, Josef, came to Dakota Territory from Moravia (Czech Republic), and the recipe has been passed down through five generations to Sandi Vojta. Today, Vojta makes more than thirty different wines from fruits of the prai-rie, as well as from domestic fruit and grapes. One of her most popular wines is still made from her great-great grandmother's chokecherry wine recipe and is named Great Grandma's Choke-cherry Bliss.

Prairie Berry Winery is housed in a soaring structure built to resemble a gold mine. The theme suits its location in the Black Hills. The area experienced a gold rush in 1876 and then became the site of the Homestake Gold Mine, which operated for one

Located in Hill City, the Prairie Berry Winery building reflects the architecture of mining facilities during the Black Hills gold rush.
Courtesy of Rodger Slott, flashbox.us

hundred twenty-five years. Black Hills gold jewelry, a popular locally designed item, features a grape-leaf motif. Prairie Berry Winery is located midway between Mount Rushmore and Crazy Horse Memorial. In the Black Hills, which contains the highest peak east of the Rocky Mountains, Mount Rushmore National Memorial towers fifty-five hundred feet above sea level and features the granite faces of presidents George Washington, Thomas Jefferson, Theodore Roosevelt, and Abraham Lincoln. Sculptor Gutzon Borglum completed the symbol of democracy in 1941. In honor of the memorial, Prairie Berry Winery has created three wines called the Wines of Democracy: Freedom, a white; Independence, a red; and Liberty, a blush wine.

In the scenic and rich cultural area of the Black Hills, another monumental sculpture rises nearby. Sculptor Korczak Ziolkowski began the Crazy Horse Memorial in 1948 as a tribute to the Lakota Sioux warrior Crazy Horse. The sculptor died in 1982, but his family continues his work. Near Hill City, too, are the historic towns of Lead, Deadwood, and Custer. Visitors to Lead can see the open pit of the former Homestake Gold

Mine and visit the Black Hills Mining Museum and Homestake Visitor Center. Deadwood, a National Historic District, was home to Wild Bill Hickok and Calamity Jane and contains many modern gambling establishments. Custer, the oldest town in the Black Hills, was the site of the first discovery of gold in French Creek. In Hill City, visitors can ride on an 1880 steam-driven train that takes passengers on a two-hour trip to Keystone and back. Each fall, Prairie Berry Winery hosts a four-course dinner aboard the train. Each course is paired with wine on this Wine Train into the West adventure.

Matt Keck and Sandi Vojta display the oak barrels used in making some wines at Prairie Berry Winery.

Throughout the year, Vojta creates new wines with the help of her husband and business manager Matt Keck, her father and assistant winemaker Ralph Vojta, marketing director Michelle Slott, and the rest of their enthusiastic staff. Prairie Berry Winery employs six full-time staff and up to thirty employees in the summer. The winery includes a gift shop, tasting room, separate meeting rooms, and an outdoor patio area. The winery has no vineyard of its own and purchases grapes, fruit, and honey from growers all over the state. "The entire state of South Dakota is our vineyard," Keck said. "Each year, Mother Nature determines what wines we will produce. We typically purchase buffalo berries, chokecherries, wild plums, and domestic fruit such as pears, raspberries, black currants, apples, and strawberries."

Prairie Berry produces close to fifty thousand gallons of wine per year in its modern facility. There are several stainless-steel fermenting tanks that hold up to four thousand gallons and can both heat and cool. "It's important to remove the heat so the wine does not ferment too quickly," Vojta said. After it is fermented, some of the wine is aged in oak barrels. At the appro-

Keck and Vojta proudly display their popular wines in front of the fireplace in their tasting room.

priate time, the wine is processed through an automated machine that fills, caps, and labels two thousand bottles per hour. Prairie Berry seals its bottles with screw caps and no longer uses corks. "There's some controversy to this," Vojta said, "but we've found the screw caps to be favorable."

Unique wine labels feature drawings by local artists. Bottles of Three Rednecks, a dry red wine blended from three grape varieties, aged in oak, feature a drawing of three ring-neck pheasants, which also represent three human "rednecks," Ralph Vojta, Matt Keck, and Sandi Vojta. Red Ass Rhubarb, a semisweet red wine made of rhubarb and raspberries, features a label with a drawing of a red donkey. Sandi Vojta claims the wine came about when her father made an error in the process that turned out well. Calamity Jane, a sweet, fruity red wine from Concord grapes, honors one of Deadwood's notorious characters. For these and other vintages, Prairie Berry Winery has won hundreds of awards in national and international competitions, including Best Fruit Wine East of the Rocky Mountains in the United States and Canada for its Red Ass Rhubarb in 2005 and 2006. Its Raspberry Honey wine won the same award in 2007 at the Wineries Unlimited Symposium.

Sandi Vojta summed up the philosophy of Prairie Berry Winery: "Our winery includes a big family in a big house. Everyone is a guest in our house." Events at the winery include a May art extravaganza, the fall wine train, and a Christmas Fezziwig Festival. The owners also host open houses and private parties. "Our wines provide a taste of the local culture," Matt Keck added. "Wine tasting is not a sterile experience. It's very cool and exciting. It's a memory in a bottle."

Wyoming

Phil Napoli plants grapevines wherever they will grow at
Rocky Ridge Vineyards, including along the edge of the buildings.
Courtesy of Phil Napoli

Rocky Ridge Vineyard Powell, Wyoming

The future of the grapevines of Rocky Ridge Vineyard is as precarious as the rocks they survive in. Strewn over seven acres south of Powell, Wyoming, the grapevines have been planted wherever they will grow. "As you come up the driveway to the house, you'll find grapevines along the road; you'll see grapevines beside the barn; you'll see grapevines wherever I can get them to survive," said owner Phil Napoli. The soil is about seventy percent rock where Napoli lives on the edge of the old Shoshone River plain. The farm is now a mile and a half from the Shoshone River, but Napoli believes it was once probably part of the riverbed.

Napoli moved to his place near Powell in 2001 with plans to garden in his retirement. He hated gardening, though, and soon looked for an alternative that would still give him the satisfaction of farming. After talking to Patrick Zimmerer of Table Mountain Vineyards in Huntley, Wyoming, and to researchers at the University of Wyoming, Napoli decided to try planting grapevines and established a varietal test plot on his acreage. "If I knew then what I know three years later, I might have changed my mind," Napoli said. Raising grapevines, he found, was just like raising cows. They have to be checked on and taken care of every day. "I go out every morning to see if the vines are still alive and nothing has eaten them," he said. When he began digging holes to plant the grapevines in 2004, Napoli said he was not able to use a posthole digger but had to dig the holes with a backhoe. He started out with one hundred vines of ten varieties of grapes, including eight red varieties and two white varieties. By 2007, the vineyard had grown to four hundred twenty-five vines and seventy varieties.

"I'm really more interested in finding out what varieties will survive in northern Wyoming than I am in just growing grapes to sell," Napoli said. He is excited about the Marquette grape, a

Grapevines grow despite the rocky soil and high winds near Powell, Wyoming. *Courtesy of Phil Napoli*

new variety released in 2006 by the University of Minnesota. "It's supposed to be very cold-hardy, resistant to disease, and easy to manage," he said. "I think it will be the grape to really give us northern wine growers a chance to market a grape that will make a good red tannic wine similar to Cabernet Sauvignon." Napoli grows other prominent varieties at Rocky Ridge Vineyard, including Frontenac, Marechal Foch, Leon Millot, Saint Croix, and Valiant. Napoli is also experimenting with some grapevines from China and Russia. He propagates cuttings from his vines and is growing some grapevines from seedlings. Napoli has had no problems with disease or pests so far. He uses an egg-and-garlic spray to discourage the deer from coming into the vineyard, and he sprays fertilizer directly on the plants because "it would take ground fertilizer a year or more to get to the roots through the rocks."

He also installed a drip-irrigation system and uses mostly vertical-shoot-position trellis systems. "It's very windy where we live, so I'm still experimenting with the proper trellis sys-

Carol and Phil Napoli taught school before trying their hand at growing grapes at Rocky Ridge Vineyard. *Courtesy of Phil Napoli*

tem," he said. "The Saint Croix vines were just beat to death by the wind, but they've come back and I hope they'll make it. In fact this whole thing is just one big experiment, and I may have bitten off more than I can chew, but what else would I do with my time now that I'm retired?"

Both Napoli and his wife, Carol, were schoolteachers in Cleveland, Ohio, before moving to Wyoming and operating a resort outside of Yellowstone National Park on the Bear Tooth Highway. The couple finally sold the facility in 2001 and moved to the acreage south of Powell, which is located seventy-five miles east of Yellowstone National Park. The vineyard is in a major agricultural district with around eighty-eight thousand acres of irrigated farmland. Water for irrigation comes from the Buffalo Bill Dam on the Shoshone River, a project that the United States Bureau of Reclamation completed in 1908. The town of Powell bears the name of Major John Wesley Powell, explorer, conservationist, and head of the reclamation/geodetic service. Because of the irrigated farmland near his acreage, Napoli believes he will be able to subirrigate his vineyard once the root systems are well developed.

"When it comes to breeding and growing grapes, I've still got more questions than answers," he admitted. He has found members of the Minnesota Grape Growers organization helpful and willing to share information, and he is a member of the Wyoming Grape and Wine Association. The grapevine test plot at the University of Wyoming experimental station at Sheridan also provides ongoing information on vine survival. Under the direction of Justin Moss, the University of Wyoming planted a new research vineyard containing thirty varieties of cold-hardy grapes at Sheridan in May 2007.

Napoli does not plan to operate a commercial winery and makes only a few gallons of wine for his own enjoyment. He has been a hobby winemaker for years and that suits him fine.

Sage Hill Vineyard Chugwater, Wyoming

A mother's vision and a daughter's determination combined to bring them back to a windy hilltop in Wyoming. At age five, Kate Koch spent an idyllic year riding horses, chasing chickens, milking cows, and playing with dogs and cats on a farm in Wyoming. Then her parents left for jobs that took them to thirteen different towns before Koch graduated from high school. Decades later, Koch's mother, Carol Eckhardt, now divorced, and her daughter found their way back to the old farmstead they had once cared for. They had not really planned it that way. A Christmas trip to visit relatives in Chugwater, Wyoming, where Eckhardt had graduated from high school, started the chain of events that led to the formation of Sage Hill Vineyard.

"Auntie Ruth told me our old farmstead, consisting of an old house and a few acres, was for sale, but she thought it had already been sold," Eckhardt said. Undaunted, Eckhardt called the owner who said that several people had looked, "but none had put any money down." He offered to show Eckhardt the place, and they drove over to see it. "The house hadn't been inhabited for five years. There was daylight showing through the roof, and most of the windows were gone," Eckhardt recalled. "I don't know why I wasn't just horrified at the condition of the house, but I wasn't. The other buyers eventually dropped out, and by September of 2002, we made a deal to buy the place." Eckhardt was working at the University of Wyoming, one hundred twenty miles away in Laramie, but spent most weekends for the next four years fixing up the farm near Chugwater. Koch was working in Casper, Wyoming, and then moved to Salt Lake City, Utah. She also visited the farm as often as possible and helped to return it to a livable condition.

"I was pondering different ways we might be able to make a sustainable living on our small acreage," Eckhardt said. She eventually wanted to retire from her university position, and

Carol Eckhardt waters a newly planted grapevine at Sage Hill Vineyard near Chugwater, Wyoming.

Koch wanted to live on a farm again. In winter 2004, Eckhardt read an article in the University of Wyoming alumni magazine that piqued her interest. Extension researcher Roger Hybner had been testing grape varieties at the university's Sheridan Research and Extension Center since 1987. He had compiled enough data to help agricultural producers on the high plains start successful vineyards and wineries. The article outlined the economic potential of Wyoming-labeled wine and listed several varieties of cold-hardy grapes that could be grown in the state. Eckhardt contacted the research station, and they sent her information about the Zimmerer family, who were growing grapes about fifty miles from Eckhardt's property. "I found out that Patrick Zimmerer was finishing his degree at the UW [University of Wyoming] campus in Laramie. I called him and he came over to talk to me and encouraged me to get into the grapevine business," she said.

In spring 2004, Eckhardt and Koch planted two hundred Frontenac and two hundred LaCrescent vines. "We didn't have a

Eckhardt's daughter, Kate Koch, and a helper plant grapevines.

clue what we were doing, but a lot of friends came over to help us, and suddenly we had a vineyard," Eckhardt said. They put grow tubes around the new vines to protect them and looked for a watering system. Koch found a supplier in Salt Lake City who gave her a good deal on a drip irrigation system. "I was laying out pipe all over the floor at his place of business. There I was in high heels and a dress making sure I knew how to put all the connections together," Koch recalled. She transported everything five hundred miles to the vineyard, where it provided about five gallons of water per vine each week. That summer the women camped out at the farm, bathed in a solar shower, and used a porta-potty. Luckily, the place had a good well, and they were able to carry water until a new pump was installed. The house had to be re-plumbed, re-wired, and painted. It also needed new windows, a septic tank, a furnace, and a water heater.

During breaks in the work, Eckhardt and Koch came up with principles for Sage Hill Vineyard and a corresponding mission statement. "Our principles are: it must be sustainable, it must give back to the land, and everything has to be in balance," Koch explained. The mission statement affirms that the vineyard is committed to organic and sustainable agriculture and to practices that enhance the productivity of the soil and biological diversity. In addition to grapes, the women also grow red raspberries and several kinds of culinary herbs, including marjoram, sage, chives, lavender, and parsley. They plan to sell the raspberries and herbs at farmers' markets and the raspberries and grapes to Table Mountain Winery in Huntley, Wyoming. They are also active in the Wyoming Grape and Wine Association and participate in the organization's annual vineyard tour each August.

The Sage Hill Vineyard is planted on an east slope and receives maximum wind protection. The rows are six feet apart on an east-west line, and the vines are five feet apart. The former crested-wheat pasture acts as ground cover. The second summer, the owners installed a two-wire trellis system. The third spring, May 2007, they planted an additional eight hundred Frontenac vines. "Our LaCrescent vines died back quite a bit in the winter, and they didn't do nearly as well as the Frontenac, so we're really sold on Frontenac in this climate," said Eckhardt, who had retired from her university position in December 2006 and spent the winter at the farm. "It was quite a winter. I had to dig out of five-foot snowdrifts. . . . The rabbits did our grapevine pruning for us. They just climbed up those snowdrifts and chewed off the vines. We also have problems with antelope and deer." Koch meanwhile transferred from Salt Lake City to southeastern Wyoming and even talked her father, Clayton Enix, into moving back to the state and joining her in purchasing a farmstead near her mother's place. Koch hopes someday to retire from her full-time job and "live off the land."

In pursuit of their own dreams, both Koch and Eckhardt actively promote the local community. They often drive the seventeen miles to the tiny town of Chugwater, where Main Street is lined with boarded-up businesses. A gas station, school,

More grapevines sit in buckets of water while workers
ready the ground at Sage Hill Vineyard.

museum, restaurant, motel, and three churches survive, as do
two major tourist attractions: an old-fashioned soda fountain
that draws in visitors from busy Interstate 25, and Chugwater
Chili, a locally owned business that packages and sells spicy
chili mixes all over the world. If only for the name itself, Chugwater appears to have great potential. According to local legend,
American Indians used to drive herds of buffalo over the bluffs
that surround the valley. As the buffalo fell to their deaths by
a stream, the Indians said they made a gurgling noise "at the
place by the water where the buffalo chug"—thence the name
Chugwater evolved. Both mother and daughter realize the

importance of their new venture to the area. "I'm surprised that grapes do grow here," Koch admitted. "We've got some rocky soil, some clay soil, dreadful wind, drought, huge snowdrifts, deer, antelope, and rabbits. It's a challenge. We hope for the best and keep on going. We are a novelty in the community and we're being watched. If we are successful, others will follow suit."

Eckhardt and Koch welcome visitors, by appointment, at Sage Hill Vineyard. They love talking about their fledgling enterprise and sharing what they have learned about growing grapes on the high plains of Wyoming. "We are living proof that you can go home again," both women say with big smiles on their faces. Under a bright blue western sky with the distant mountains off to the west, Sage Hill Vineyard is a testament to the many pioneer women who have dared to dream.

Table Mountain Vineyards Huntley, Wyoming

When the Zimmerer family of Huntley, Wyoming, planted their first three hundred grapevines, they were advised to limit the care of the new vines in order to make them suffer. The conventional wisdom was that grapevines thrived best when made to struggle. "I thought bringing them to Wyoming was making them suffer enough," chuckled Patrick Zimmerer, whose family had homesteaded in southeastern Wyoming in the 1920s. They settled in the Platte River Valley in Goshen County, close to the Nebraska border, where soft rolling hills made of sandy soil form the center of a large bowl known as Goshen Hole. Sandstone bluffs rim the area, formed by a dried-up ancient lake. American Indians found the valley a pleasant place to winter, and early emigrants following the Oregon and Mormon trails crossed this area on their approach to the Rocky Mountains. Just southeast of the Zimmerer farm is a long flat butte named Table Mountain.

In 2001, Bruce and Lorie Zimmerer raised cattle, hay, corn, and sugar beets. They were looking for a crop to replace sugar beets because the income from the crop was declining. Their son, Patrick, was completing his senior year at the University of Wyoming when he hit upon an idea for his senior research project. "I was home on Christmas break and attended a workshop in Scottsbluff, Nebraska, on viticulture," he recalled. Growing grapes sounded interesting, he thought, and when he got back to school, he told his agricultural economics professor that he wanted to do his senior paper on the feasibility of growing grapes in eastern Wyoming and western Nebraska. He attended a spring pruning clinic in Nebraska and was further convinced that a vineyard would be a great project that could provide income for the family farm. His senior paper showed that it could be a profitable venture. The sandy soil on their farm was ideal for growing grapes, and the University of Minnesota had

Elvira grapevines grow in the foreground at Table Mountain Vineyards near Huntley, Wyoming. In the background, Table Mountain rises above the plains.

developed several grape varieties that were compatible with the cold weather of the high plains area.

"We were really enthused about the project," said Bruce Zimmerer. "The only problem was we started looking in April for grapevines to plant in May, and we had a hard time finding any vines. We finally located one hundred vines each of Valiant, Saint Croix, and Seyval Blanc." The entire family, including Patrick's sister Amie and his grandmother Donna Thompson, helped plant the first grapevines. They dug some of the holes by hand and found that they were not deep enough for the three-to-four-foot roots. The family finally borrowed a post-hole digger to deepen the holes. Thompson mowed between the rows with a lawn mower and hoed around the vines during the first growing season. They watered the vines with a garden hose. "We lost the Saint Croix vines because they had been improperly stored at the nursery, but the other vines grew and did well," Patrick Zimmerer said.

The project was so successful the first year that the family decided to plant an additional two thousand vines the second year. They planted all the vines in one weekend and found it worked best to use a mechanical digger to make the holes. The planters followed behind, supporting each vine with a six-foot bamboo pole. They planted in rows eight feet apart and spaced the vines six feet apart. A drip irrigation system supplied five gallons of water per vine per week. The family installed a trellis system to anchor the vines, using wooden posts set between every four vines with two wires passing horizontally through each post. The vines were eventually trained to form four branches with two branches supported on each of the horizontal wires. It is painful in the spring, Patrick Zimmerer explained, when "you have to prune those vines you worked so hard to get to grow back to three buds near the ground level. If you don't prune them, you won't get the growth you want to produce fruit, and the vines are unmanageable."

In 2003, the family added the popular variety Frontenac, especially developed to grow in the cold, harsh plains. "We

Patrick Zimmerer explains the operation of a grape press at Table Mountain Vineyards.

couldn't buy any of the Frontenac vines up to that point, they were always sold out," Bruce Zimmerer said. They also added LaCrescent, Frontenac Gris, and Elvira vines. In the planning stages, the Zimmerers had talked to a winery owner in Cheyenne about buying their grapes, "but, when we harvested our first crop in 2004, that winery had gone out of business," Patrick Zimmerer recalled. "We thought, how hard can it be to make wine? So we plunged right into our next adventure, making our own wine. I had spent three years at law school after planting the first vines, and it takes three years to get a grape crop, so I figured it must be fate that we should start a winery."

Patrick Zimmerer and his sister Amie submitted a business plan for their winery to a competition and won the top prize of ten thousand dollars. They used the money to renovate an old farmhouse, where the family had lived for twenty years, for use as a winery. The small tan stucco house by the side of a dusty track is a far cry from the winery mansions of California, but it suits the Wyoming prairie. To become a winemaker, Patrick

During harvest, a worker uses a grapefork to pick grapes.

Zimmerer attended several seminars in Nebraska and Minnesota. The family also obtained the proper permits and bought some basic hobby winemaker supplies. They made the first wine in fourteen-gallon containers and used a small crusher to process the grapes. In 2004, they used three hundred pounds of their own Valiant grapes and some Frontenac grapes from a nearby grower, Del Bass of Torrington, to make wine. "It takes sixteen pounds of grapes to make one gallon of wine," Patrick Zimmerer said. "Each grapevine produces ten to thirty pounds of grapes."

In 2005, they purchased a larger crusher and struggled to move it through the front door of the winery. After taking it apart, the Zimmerers installed it in the former living room of the old farmhouse. They also added several forty-eight-gallon plastic barrels for fermenting. "We aren't professional winemakers by any standard," Patrick Zimmerer said. "We focus on using a 100-percent Wyoming product as far as possible. We also don't add a lot of chemicals, although we sometimes add a few oak chips to the fermenting barrels. We use the philosophy of fruit forward in our wines, letting the fruit speak for itself. We want our wines to be full of Wyoming character." Table Mountain Vineyards also produces wines from Wyoming honey, apples, and raspberries. The first wines were bottled in January and February 2005.

The Zimmerers' marketing strategy has been to host open-house events and participate in wine-tastings and festivals. Pat-

The electronic grape crusher, on the left, removes the grape stems and sends the crushed mixture, called must, through a hose into the barrels on the right, where it undergoes primary fermentation. Vintners help each other during the busy season, and Jackie Hopken, of South Fork Vineyard in Nebraska, helps crush grapes at Table Mountain Vineyards in Wyoming.

rick Zimmerer also helped form the Wyoming Grape and Wine Association and serves as president. The Zimmerers' wine labels include Prairie Gold and Sweet Bee, honey wines; Wyo Wine O, apple wine; Cowboy Reserve, grape wine from Marechal Foch grapes; S.O.B. (son of berry), raspberry wine; RAZ, raspberry dessert wine; Rooster Red, from Valiant grapes; and Frontenac, from Frontenac grapes. In 2005, the Table Mountain Vineyards Rooster Red wine label was featured in an exhibit of wine labels from each state at the Smithsonian Museum in Washington, D.C. The limited supply of wine sold out within one month.

Along with the triumphs, there have been challenges. Disaster hit Table Mountain Vineyards in July 2006, when a devastating hailstorm stripped the leaves from every grapevine. "I thought we'd lost all the vines, but they did recover quite a bit. We ended up losing about 45 percent of the crop," Zimmerer said. Another problem has been the Wyoming liquor laws. Established in the early 1900s, the laws permitted no retail sales of wines except through the state liquor commission. "We were so small our wine got lost in the liquor warehouse in Cheyenne,"

Patrick Zimmerer said. In 2005, the state law was changed to allow Wyoming wineries to ship wine to in-state retailers and consumers. "We can also ship out-of-state, depending on the laws of that state. There is usually a fee to ship out-of-state, and sometimes the fee is prohibitive if we only have a small amount to ship," Zimmerer said. "In fact, here we are a mile from the Nebraska state line, and we have to pay too much to ship there. I never thought that state line would be so difficult to cross."

In spring 2007, Zimmerer helped establish the Wines on the Historic Trails route, featuring the wines of southeastern Wyoming and western Nebraska. "Each winery on the trail is focused on making fruit-forward style wines," he said. The businesses on the trail are: Table Mountain Winery in Huntley, Wyoming; Prairie Vine Winery in Mitchell, Nebraska; 17 Ranch Winery in Lewellen, Nebraska; and South Fork Vineyard in Ogallala, Nebraska. Like pioneers on an overland trail, modern-day travelers who take this route can find a place to rest, something to quench their thirst, and friendly conversation. At Table Mountain Vineyards, the path includes a few miles travel on a gravel road, but the tasting room is open for scheduled tours and by appointment and feels as comfortable as one's own living room.

Bass Farm Torington, Wyoming

An old corral, a pile of junk, and a California dream provided the inspiration for the first commercial vineyard in Wyoming. It was a long journey for Del Bass, who grew up on a ranch near Jay Em, Wyoming, earned a degree in geology from the University of Wyoming, and left the state for an international career in the oil business. During a stint in Africa, he met his wife Janet, a native of England. The couple ultimately returned to the United States and bought an irrigated farm near Torrington in 1976. "I was desperate to own land in Wyoming," Bass recalled. The couple moved to the farm in 1989 after Del Bass retired. "It all started with an ugly old feed lot and a junk pile that we decided we needed to clean up," he said. "We'd just returned from a trip to northern California where I fell in love with the vineyards," Janet Bass added. She noticed that grapes grew on sandy, rocky soil there, and she figured they should be able to do the same in Wyoming. "Of course," she said, "I forgot that we have harsher winters in Wyoming."

Del Bass thought that growing wine grapes would be a good idea despite the climate differences. They cleaned up the corral and hired someone to level the ground. They had the soil tested and found that it contained the correct amount of nutrients with a good pH balance to grow grapes. Bass joined the Minnesota Grape Growers Association after he learned that Minnesota had an active group of vintners growing cold-weather-variety grapes. He also attended a grape and wine seminar in Nebraska and consulted with Paul Read of the University of Nebraska, who assured him it was possible to grow grapes in Wyoming. "In fact, Wyoming has an ideal climate for grapes, except for the winters. Grapes like well-drained soil and lots of sun. The dry climate also eliminates problems such as mildew and pests that plague growers in wetter climates," Bass said.

Janet and Del Bass prune a vine at their vineyard.

After cleaning up their acreage, the couple planted grass. They wanted a low-maintenance vineyard, and grass eliminated the weeds. In 1999, the couple planted fifty-two vines of Marechal Foch and what they thought were Valiant grapes. The nursery, however, mixed up the order. "Three years later when we had some white grapes mixed in with the red grapes, we found out we'd also planted Edelweiss grapes," Del Bass recalled. He also planted twenty-six Frontenac vines after he learned that the grapes had a good reputation for growing in cold climates. "I have learned to really like Frontenac vines because they bud a little later in the spring than other varieties, and they also bud in stages. If we get a late frost in May, it won't kill all the buds and some will come out a little later," he said. In 2002, a late freeze killed the Marechal Foch and Edelweiss vines. Bass dug them up and replaced them with Frontenac, adding enough vines to total one hundred, including five Valiant vines. He considers Valiant to be an excellent hardy variety but not the best producer. The first grapes were harvested in 2003 and

Del Bass moves along the well-tended rows of vines at Bass Farm.

delivered to Table Mountain Vineyards at Huntley, Wyoming, because the Basses do not make their own wine. The harvest averaged around eight pounds per vine, but some produced as much as twenty pounds.

In order to protect the vineyard from Wyoming's harsh winds, Del Bass built a solid fence on the west side of the vineyard and planted clematis to cover the fence, along with a row of cedar trees and a row of bushes. On the east side, he planted a row of English black currants in memory of his wife's home in England. Bass uses a one-wire trellis to support the vines and puts plastic ground cover under the rows to keep down the weeds. He irrigates with drip irrigation and applies ten gallons of water per vine once a week during the summer months. After the grapes begin to ripen in August, he covers the vines with netting to protect them from the birds, which seem to "really enjoy eating grapes." He does not use any fertilizer but does use a chemical to control beetles and flies. Because corn fields surround the Bass farm, he is concerned about the substances other farmers spray on their crops, but the grapes have sustained only a small amount of damage from the chemicals that Bass says are "deadly for grapevines."

Janet Bass assists in the vineyard and works full-time as an academic coordinator for the University of Wyoming. She writes for regional newspapers and agricultural publications and serves as secretary of the Wyoming Grape and Wine Association. Del and Janet Bass are delighted to share what they have learned about growing grapes on the Wyoming plains and welcome visitors to make an appointment to tour the vineyard.

Nebraska

This mural, painted on the side of the winery,
appears on the Prairie Vine labels and evokes
the beauty of western Nebraska.

Prairie Vine Vineyard and Winery

Mitchell, Nebraska

Years of drought, low farm prices, children who were not interested, and a divorce forced Allen Gall to look at farming from a different perspective. "I used to be a really big farmer with over a thousand acres of land planted in sugar beets, corn, and hay. I also raised cattle. All but eighty acres of the farm was on leased land. My sons went away to college, and one became an artist, the other a veterinarian. They didn't want to farm and I knew I couldn't do it all by myself. I thought there has to be a way to make a living on eighty acres," Gall said. Gall experimented with planting grass to feed cattle, but he did not have enough acres, and drought prevented the seed from sprouting. His agricultural extension agent from the University of Nebraska suggested he try planting grapes. "Grapes!" Gall said. "Wow, that would be a lot of work, and I'd probably get laughed out of the county." A few months later, Gall and the extension agent attended a football game in Lincoln. "My agent took me over to the James Arthur Vineyard and Winery at Raymond, just north of Lincoln. I fell in love with that place and decided I wanted a winery. And, of course, I'd need some grapes if I wanted a winery," Gall said.

He planted thirty-five hundred vines on seven acres in the spring of 2000. The vineyard now grows Brianna, Edelweiss, Saint Croix, Marechal Foch, De Chaunac, LaCrosse, and Traminette grapes. Gall's favorite vine is the Saint Croix because it produces a prolific red grape. He planted four hundred eighty-eight vines on one acre and harvested two and a half tons to the acre. Gall has planted his vine rows twelve feet apart with a vine every eight feet. He uses a two-wire trellis system to support the vines and a drip irrigation system. He has installed netting above his vineyard to protect it from birds and has had trouble with raccoons that "just love those sweet grapes."

During the three years the grapes were growing, Gall attended several winemaking schools. "Winemaking is an extra challenge for me because I'm allergic to alcohol," he said. Allowing the fruit to determine flavor, he compensates with his nose. "I can smell the bouquet of the wine, and if it's not a good smell I know it's not a good wine." Gall ferments his wines in stainless-steel tanks, usually allowing about four weeks for white wine and a little longer for red. He sometimes ages a few grape varieties in oak barrels. In December 2004, Gall opened his winery just off the main highway through Mitchell, Nebraska. In the modest, one-story, blue-steel building, he produced fifteen hundred cases of wine in 2005 and 2006. The winery's reception area is furnished with antiques and tables for guests and includes a gift shop. Gall's mother, Carlene, manages the winery and gift shop. His future plans include a new winery with a forty-eight-hundred-square-foot production and reception area. The winery will be located between Mitchell and Scottsbluff just off state Highway 26 on Sunflower Oil Road. "I'm planting more grapes in that area, too, so that visitors can see a vineyard when they visit the winery," Gall said. Currently, his vineyard is several miles away, but "most people like to see the grapevines, too."

Except for picking the grapes, Gall does most of the vineyard work himself. "We harvest all by hand and get help wherever we can find it: friends, relatives, church youth groups, and just about anyone interested in helping out. We pay the youth groups so they use it as a fund-raiser, and I think they have a lot of fun, too," he said. The harvest runs from about the third week of August to the first week of October. "It can get a little crazy during harvest. I don't get much sleep," said Gall. He buys some grapes from other growers, who deliver at the same time Gall is harvesting his own grapes. "I've got one guy that will bring me a load of grapes at midnight, and they've got to be processed right away or they'll go to waste." In spite of the hours, Gall loves

Owner and winemaker Allen Gall stirs a vat of fruit
at Prairie Vine Winery near Mitchell, Nebraska.

the whole process, especially the winery. He makes most of his
wine from locally grown grapes, but he also uses other fruits
such as apples, raspberries, blackberries, and blueberries.

Prairie Vine Winery markets over a dozen wines, most of
which are named for historic landmarks in the area. Monument
Red, a dry red wine, is named for Scotts Bluff Monument. Roubadeau Red, a red wine made from Frontanac grapes, honors the

pioneers who made it through Roubadeau Pass. Chimney Rock Red, a semisweet red wine made from the Saint Croix grape, carries the name of another local landmark. Platte River Red is a sweet red wine made from a blend of grapes grown in the Platte River Valley. Visitors to the winery can see Chimney Rock and Scotts Bluff rising above the Platte River Valley. These sandstone bluffs served as natural landmarks for emigrants traveling the Oregon, California, and Mormon trails. The bluffs, stretching for about thirty-five miles from east to west, rise eight hundred feet above the North Platte River and were visible for days before travelers reached them. At Scotts Bluff, the geology of the badlands forced travelers out of the river valley and through a narrow area they named Roubadeau Pass.

Gall has joined with other winery owners in western Nebraska and eastern Wyoming to form the Wines on the Historic Trails route. The trail follows Highway 26 and features the monuments and bluffs and other stops along the old Pony Express, Oregon, California, and Mormon trails. Having embarked on a new adventure raising grapes and making wine at midlife, Gall reminds modern travelers, however, "There's nothing prettier than a vineyard, unless it's a herd of cows."

17 **Ranch Winery** Lewellen, Nebraska

When ranch woman Ellen Burdick made up her mind to start a winery, she let nothing stand in her way. Several years ago this co-owner of the 17 Ranch in western Nebraska decided to grow grapes. "It all started when I read a letter to the editor in the *Garden County News* in February 1999, talking about the profitability of growing grapes in Nebraska," Burdick said. "I started making phone calls to find out more information, and by May, my husband Bruce and I decided to plant one acre of land, consisting of four hundred fifty-five vines, into grapevines." They planted Frontenac, Marechal Foch, Saint Vincent, LaCrosse, and Edelweiss the first year, adding Traminette vines later. "By 2007, we had four acres of vines," she said.

The land where the vineyard sits was formerly a cornfield. "Corn was selling for three cents a pound in 1999, and grapes were selling for fifty to sixty cents a pound. It made sense to switch from corn to grapes even though it takes three years to get a grape crop," Burdick said. "Of course, now that corn is being used for ethanol that equation may change." Burdick's grapevines are watered about four times during the growing season from a nearby ditch that also irrigates other crops on the ranch. "Another advantage of grapevines is that they don't take near the water that corn does," she added.

Bruce Burdick and a high-school student care for the grapevines, which are on a vertical-shoot-position trellis, except for the Edelweiss, which is on a high-cordon trellis. "We get a lot of wind here, so those trellis systems seem to work the best for us," Ellen Burdick explained. She also installs bird netting when the grapes are mature. "We use quarter-mile-long panels, and it takes three people about fifteen minutes to put on a quarter mile of the netting that we roll from the back of a vehicle while driving along the grapevine row," she said. She frightens deer away from the vineyard by clipping fabric softener squares to

Ranch woman Ellen Burdick examines the vines at her 17 Ranch Vineyard near Lewellen, Nebraska

the trellis every few feet. The Burdicks use no fertilizer and a minimal amount of spray for mildew and have allowed grass to grow between the vine rows.

Ellen Burdick was pleased with the first harvest of one hundred eighty pounds of grapes in 2002, and production has increased every year since then. She was not satisfied with selling the grapes to another winery, however, and started thinking about making her own wine. "People thought I was just talking when I said I was going to open a winery," she recalled. "They said it would never happen." When her aging parents passed away, she found the experience bittersweet because it freed up the time "to do the homework required to start a winery," Burdick said. She had to remodel a building for the winery and obtain federal and state licenses. "Everyone told me it takes at least six months to get licensed. Well, like I said, I did my homework and found out what I needed to do to submit a perfect application for my license. I sent the application in on June 5, 2006, and on August 1, 2006, I had my license. It was unheard of to get a license in less than 60 days," Burdick said. "But, when I make up my mind to do something, I get it done."

Burdick took several classes, including the entrepreneur training program sponsored by the Nebraska Cooperative Extension Service and learned to write a business plan. She also took several winemaking classes and a two-day workshop at Whiskey Run Creek Winery in Brownville, Nebraska. The book *From Vines to Wines: The Complete Guide to Growing Grapes and Making Your Own Wine*, by Jeff Cox, also proved to be extremely valuable. Burdick credits husband Bruce with providing both manual labor and moral support for the enterprise. "He's incredibly well organized and kept me going on the right track many times," she said. "We both also had to work hard to keep up the crop and livestock portion of the ranch while starting the vineyard and winery."

Burdick found a building on Main Street in Lewellen that could be converted into a winery. On 23 June 2006, she traveled to Austin, Texas, to buy the equipment for the production facility. The remodeling was completed on 1 July 2006, and by 15 August, Burdick was processing her first batch of grapes. In the new winery, Burdick installed ten stainless-steel tanks, a crusher nicknamed "Lucy," and a juice press. She also has a laboratory. "It's very important to test and measure everything when making wine," she said. "I make Nebraska wine with a fresh fruit-forward quality. It seems to suit the midwestern palate."

Some of the favorite wines produced at 17 Ranch Winery include Trail Dust, a dry rose wine from Frontenac grapes, and Windmill's Song, a semidry white wine made from Traminette grapes. Bruce Burdick named the wine after the sound of windmills. Prairie Sandreed, a semisweet red wine made from Saint Vincent grapes, is named for the grass that grows in the Nebraska sandhills. Ash Hollow Gold, a white wine made from Edel-

On a ladder, Burdick checks the wine fermenting in a tank.

weiss grapes, carries the name of nearby Ash Hollow, where travelers on the Oregon Trail used to stop. Wine labels from 17 Ranch Winery include a picture of a windmill, a rope, and a bull, all reflecting the pioneer heritage of the area. Travelers on the Oregon Trail, which stretched for two thousand miles from Missouri to Oregon, followed the trail along the Platte River in Nebraska. As pioneers approached the Lewellen area, they had to descend a steep hill to reach Ash Hollow, where they were rewarded with abundant fresh water and shade. After passing through what is now Lewellen, the Oregon Trail led westward to Courthouse Rock, Jail Rock, Chimney Rock, and Scotts Bluff.

The 17 Ranch Winery has joined with other vineyards and wineries in western Nebraska and eastern Wyoming in the Wines on the Historic Trails promotion. The trail begins in Ogallala, Nebraska, at the South Fork Vineyard, then leads to the 17

In her laboratory, Burdick measures the amount of sugar in her honey wine.

Ranch Winery in Lewellen, the Prairie Vine Vineyard in Mitchell, and Table Mountain Winery in Huntley, Wyoming. Visitors to 17 Ranch Winery can stay at the ranch bed and breakfast, dine on home cooking, and participate in bird watching and horseback riding. Special events include live music, art exhibits, and private parties. Entertainment featuring western heritage is planned for each month.

PRAIRIE LAKES COUNTRY

South Fork Vineyard Ogallala, Nebraska

The day the trail marker was hammered into the ground was an exciting one at South Fork Vineyard just south of Ogallala, Nebraska. The blue marker commemorated the spot where the Oregon Trail, California Trail, and Pony Express Trail intersected. From the 1840s through the 1860s, emigrants followed the Oregon and California trails to the west coast. The Pony Express carried mail along the same route from Saint Joseph, Missouri, to Sacramento, California. Ogallala was the end of the trail for cowboys driving herds of longhorns up from Texas for shipment east on the Union Pacific Railroad. Rod and Jackie Hopken, owners of South Fork Vineyard, were delighted to have the trail marker placed at the entrance to their small farm. "It was one more chance to educate visitors about the history of the West as well as to tell them about the new history we are creating by growing grapes in Nebraska," Jackie Hopken explained.

The Hopkens decided to enter the vineyard business after reading a story in the local newspaper about Ellen Burdick of 17 Ranch Winery in nearby Lewellen, Nebraska. "My husband, Rod, called Ellen's husband, Bruce, to ask about the vineyard, and we decided it would be an ideal project to fit in with our farm tours," Jackie Hopken said. "We planted our first six hundred sixty grapevines consisting of Marechal Foch, Kay Gray, and Valiant varieties in May 2000. In 2001, we added a row of table grapes, and in 2002, we planted Traminette and De Chaunac vines. We took out the Traminette in 2007, though, as it didn't do well in our sandy soil with a high pH level," she added.

The Hopkens attended meetings of the Nebraska Wine and Grape Growers Association and the Governor's Conference on Agri-Tourism to learn what visitors expect from an educational tour of a vineyard. To their property, they also added a gazebo and a pergola (a covered area with picnic tables), where they host parties, weddings, and other events that attract visitors.

A sign marks the convergence of the Oregon Trail, the California Trail, and the Pony Express Trail near Ogallala, Nebraska, and the entrance of South Fork Vineyard.

Jackie Hopken of South Fork Vineyard leads educational tours in her "vin-car."

In a typical tour, Jackie Hopken loads visitors into her "vin-car," an old Chevy with the top cut off and tools tucked in the open trunk area. As she drives through the vineyard rows, she tells her audience about how the grapes were planted, how they are tended by pruning, and how they are harvested in the late summer and early fall. "We try to keep things as natural as possible. The ground cover between the vine rows is brome grass. We don't use fertilizer or chemicals. We use a three-wire trellis and put netting over the mature grapes to keep out the birds," she explains.

Jackie is also a beekeeper and tends twenty hives kept in a nearby field of alfalfa. She extracts and processes the honey in her "honey house," making honey products such as soaps, lip balm, hand lotion, candles, and flavored cream honeys. Tours also include a visit to the honey house to see how honey is extracted, and in mid-September, visitors are invited to extract their own honey from the honeycomb. Guests can also see and pet farm animals, including llamas, goats, ducks, chickens, and peacocks. Rod Hopken often hitches the draft horses, Sam and Babe, to a wagon and gives visitors a ride around the farmyard. At harvest time, customers interested in learning the process can come to the vineyard and pick their own grapes for wines, jellies, juices, or just for eating. Most of the grapes are sold to

Hopken surveys the neat rows of her vineyard near Ogallala, Nebraska.

other wineries. Tent camping is available, and a wide pasture is set aside for kite flying.

South Fork Vineyards is the first stop on the Wines on the Historic Trails promotion from the Nebraska Department of Economic Development. At the convergence of three trails, visitors can imagine jostling along in a covered wagon or riding on a pony to deliver the mail to the next Pony Express station. By visiting a modern vineyard, they can experience both the Old and the New West.

Three Brothers Vineyard and Winery
Farnham, Nebraska

The original three brothers, Herman, Otto, and Freidrich Wach, are no longer living, but some of their descendants have decided to carry on with their agricultural roots. The Wach brothers, Germans from Russia, arrived at Ellis Island, New York, in June 1885, the same day the Statue of Liberty arrived in America. The brothers farmed in central Nebraska, where they met and married the three Schulz sisters, Anna, Johanna, and Emilie. Each couple raised large families. One of their grandsons, Gary Wach, honored his forebears by naming his enterprise Three Brothers Vineyard and Winery, although the winery has not yet opened. "This is where we have chosen to live; we wanted to stay here and raise our family, so we needed to find a way to use the land wisely and supplement our income," Gary Wach's wife, Ricky Sue, said in explaining their reasons for starting a vineyard.

Gary and Ricky Sue Wach both teach at the Nebraska College of Technical Agriculture in nearby Curtis, where Gary teaches agricultural mechanics and Ricky Sue is a veterinarian. Like so many others in the rural West, the Wachs searched for ways to provide economic diversity to their communities. They attended meetings on economic development, consulted with educators at various colleges and universities, and became interested in the possibility of growing grapes on the ten acres they had purchased on the outskirts of Farnham, Nebraska. They both completed an entrepreneur training program sponsored by the University of Nebraska Cooperative Extension Service and a program for promoting tourism to communities sponsored by the University of Nebraska Rural Initiative project. "We both wanted to work outdoors. We thought about planting an orchard, but that takes even longer than the three or four years

Gary Wach oversees
the vines at Three Brothers
Vineyard near Farnham.

it takes a vineyard to produce a crop, so we decided to plant grapes," Gary Wach said.

The couple started out with three hundred vines on one acre in 2001 and now have twenty-seven hundred vines on five acres. "It's a lot of work, but we really do enjoy being in the vineyard," Ricky Sue Wach said. "It's a great benefit to have Gary's mechanical knowledge. He used several improvised farm implements to dig the holes for the grapevines, install the trellises, and in the ongoing vineyard management." Like nearly all vintners, they have problems controlling deer, rodents, and birds. Gary Wach put aluminum cans on the tops of the steel posts that hold the wires for the vineyard trellises in an attempt to frighten birds. "The reflection from the cans does help some, but we'll still have to put up netting when the grapes mature," he said. "It gives me a nice surface to rest the netting on as I string it along the top of the vineyard canopy." The Wachs installed a drip irrigation system and use some pesticides to control weeds, bugs, and fungus. The new grapes are watered each day, but the older vines are watered every three weeks. "We use less water on the vines than we do to water our lawn," Ricky Sue Wach said.

The vineyard grows Frontenac, Frontenac Gris, LaCrosse, Landot, Brianna, Marechal Foch, Vingoles, Seyval, and Rougean grapes, but Gary Wach is fondest of the Landot. "The fruit has

Ice coats the vines following a storm, giving mute testimony to the hard winters of Nebraska and the hardiness of the cold-weather grapes. *Courtesy of Gary Wach*

the most beautiful deep red color, it's sweet and a good eating grape," he said. The Frontenac grape is the hardiest and easiest to grow, though it is more difficult to make good wine from the grapes. "We have some problems with cane borer pests, but the Frontenac vines seems to resist them," he said. Wach prefers to make wine from the Seyval grape and also likes the Brianna variety. "It smells like you're walking through a field of pineapples when the Brianna grapes ripen," he said. Ricky Sue Wach enjoys cooking with the grapes and occasionally makes pie from the Frontenac and Seyval varieties. "I don't remove the seeds, I just bake them into the pie, and they are sort of crunchy and nut-like. Everyone seems to like the pie," she added. She mixes five cups of de-stemmed grapes with 1 1/2 cups of sugar, 1/4 cup flour, 1 teaspoon of lemon juice, and a dash of salt. She then places the grape mixture into a pastry-lined pie pan, dots it with butter, covers with a top crust, and bakes 35 to 45 minutes at 425 degrees.

The Wachs hope to open a winery in the near future. In the meantime, the couple participates in local events, including the town carnival, German Festival, Founders Day, county fairs, and the forty-mile-long Trail to Treasure garage sale, usually held the first weekend in June, which takes visitors through many small towns in the area. They also intend to host post-plant-

Landot grapes are one of the varieties
grown at Three Brothers Vineyard and
Gary Wach's favorite.

ing parties and a harvest festival. A deck on the west side of the winery facility faces a pond, fields, and rolling grassland hills. "One of our greatest assets is our gorgeous sunsets. Visitors will be able to sit on the deck and enjoy wine and the sunset," Gary Wach said.

The Wachs are committed to promoting Farnham and its businesses, which include a bar/cafe, stained-glass artist, quilt shop, taxidermist, and veterinary clinic. There is a nearby American Indian museum with a medicine wheel and an earth lodge. "No, we won't save the little town of Farnham with our winery," Ricky Sue Wach said, but they do hope to bring people to visit and then "encourage other people to try their hand in providing something unique for tourists and locals to experience."

SANDHILLS

Harmony Vineyard Valentine, Nebraska

In the rolling, grass-covered Nebraska Sandhills where buffalo and cattle once grazed, a vineyard now covers the hillsides. The hills are actually sand dunes stabilized by the grass that holds them in place. The Lakota Sioux and Pawnee Indians once came to the area to hunt buffalo and graze their horses on the lush grass. Other people settled there to raise livestock, crops, and families in the town of Valentine and the nearby community of Harmony. Ron and Sandy Billings never thought they would own a farm, but they seized the opportunity in 2000 to buy the homestead that Sandy Billings's great-grandfather, Cyrus Van Metre, had settled. The property included an old dugout built in 1884, a house made from prairie sandstone, a home that was once officer's quarters at Fort Niobrara (moved piece by numbered piece and reassembled), and a one-hundred-year-old barn with roof beams open to the sky. After doing some research, the couple decided to try growing grapes, and they named their enterprise Harmony Vineyards for the community in which Van Metre had homesteaded.

Valentine, the nearest town, is situated in the heart of the Nebraska Sandhills atop the Ogallala aquifer, an important source of groundwater. The Billingses thought the land could be a great place to grow grapes. Sandy soil that drains well is considered ideal for grapevines, and the rolling hills look similar to the California grape-growing regions. In 2003, the Billingses jumped into the grape business, planting four thousand vines with the help of family and friends. They found out that it was not as easy as they imagined. Nebraska can suffer a hard freeze as late as mid-May, and they lost many of their vines to such a freeze in 2004. "I walked quite a ways crying that day," Sandy Billings said. "The grapes were our retirement plan that we hoped would keep us out of rocking chairs, but maybe they will put us in rocking chairs," she added with a laugh. Many family

Sandy Billings and her son, Coby, stand near the grapevines at Harmony Vineyards, where they employ the no-till method.

members and friends returned to help replant the vines, using a tree planter. Harmony Vineyard's grape varieties include Edelweiss, Marechal Foch, Frontenanc, Frontenac Gris, LaCrescent, LaCrosse, Saint Croix, and Louise Swenson, all considered to be cold-hardy.

The Billingses installed a drip irrigation system to water the grapes and left the existing vegetation in place, using a no-till method. However, the land had been farmed in the past, which means they have weeds to control. "Other critters, like deer, gophers, and birds, like to munch on grapevines or eat the grapes, too," Sandy Billings added. The Billingses' son Coby helps out as much as possible when he is not tending his own farm, raising fish, or guiding hunters. "When you work with nature, you learn a lot," Coby said. "In 2006, the birds ate quite a few of the grapes from the Frontenac Gris vines," leading the family to put up netting to keep out the birds. Each summer and fall, local middle-school students help prune vines, care for the vineyard, and assist with harvest. The Billingses have no plans to make their own wine and intend to sell their grapes to wineries in Nebraska or South Dakota.

Grapevines grow successfully at Harmony Vineyards in the Nebraska Sandhills. *Courtesy of Harmony Vineyards*

Visitors to Harmony Vineyards can also travel the historic Cowboy Trail, the nation's longest continuous recreational trail, stretching 321 miles from Norfolk to Chadron, Nebraska. The graveled trail follows the gentle hills and curves of an abandoned railroad. At nearby Fort Niobrara National Wildlife Refuge, there are hiking trails that lead to secluded canyons and waterfalls along the river. Out in the sandhills north of Valentine, Harmony is still home to descendants of those early pioneers and other families. In one little cove of sea green hills, row upon row of grapevines struggle to produce their own history at Harmony Vineyards.

Mac's Creek Vineyards and Winery

Lexington, Nebraska

At Mac's Creek Vineyards and Winery, it is all in the name. The twelve-acre vineyard lies along the banks of Spring Creek in the heart of the Platte River Valley north of Lexington, Nebraska. Members of the family-owned enterprise originally wanted to use the name Spring Creek, but their attorney suggested Mac's Creek after a stream near his boyhood home in Missouri. Since the vineyard and winery are owned and operated by the McFarland family and several generations of McFarland men had gone by the nickname Mac, "the name Mac's Creek was a perfect fit," said co-owner and winemaker Max McFarland. But it was not the only time the name Spring Creek would be discarded. In 2005, MacFarland's Spring Creek Mist wine won double gold at a California wine competition. A mention in a national wine magazine caught the attention of one of California's largest winemakers. "I thought it was pretty neat to receive a letter from Gallo Wines," McFarland recalled, "until I read the entire letter. Gallo was going to sue us for infringing on the name of Spring Creek, which is one of their copyrighted names." To avoid trouble, McFarland shortened the wine's name to Spring Mist. "We love to tell people we're a threat to Gallo Winery," McFarland said with a chuckle.

When Max and Theresa McFarland bought the twelve-acre farm that had once been a commercial feedlot, it was covered with weeds. They burned the weeds, then plowed and tilled the land before the first grapevines were planted. Like many other new grape growers, the McFarlands originally thought they would just plant a few vines and sell the grapes to other wineries. They planted one hundred vines in the spring of 2000, and the next year added one hundred more. Soon, the vineyard covered several acres, and the McFarlands decided to put a winery in a spot where the grapes did not grow well. Even though the

Winemaker Seth McFarland examines grapevines at Mac's Creek Vineyards and Winery near Lexington, Nebraska.

McFarlands are both professors at the University of Nebraska in Kearney, they consider themselves "farm kids at heart." As the enterprise grew, the McFarlands enlisted the help of their adult children, Barry, Seth, and Abbey, who are all co-owners. Max and Seth McFarland are the winemakers; Barry McFarland handles the business end; Abbey McFarland manages the gift shop; and Theresa McFarland is the tasting-room manager.

Like many other new vintners in Nebraska and surrounding states, the McFarlands traveled to other wineries in search of advice and knowledge. They appreciated the help given by Ed Swanson of Cuthills Vineyard, who established Nebraska's first

Barry and Seth McFarland designed this winery building at Mac's Creek.

vineyard and winery. "I showed up at a lot of vineyards with a tape measure, marking cones, and a notebook," Max McFarland said. "I also dragged along my high-school shop teacher from Eddyville, Gary Kuebler, because I wanted him to build the winery." While the two men were out roaming the countryside, sons Barry and Seth McFarland were at home designing the winery building on a computer. "With a few modifications to their design and the information Gary and I had gathered, we ended up with a great winery building," Max McFarland said.

The McFarlands began making wine with a small crusher and press, a refrigerated dairy tank, and a few oak barrels. Then the family decided to invest in state-of-the-art winemaking

Winemaker Max McFarland stands near the winery's
state-of-the-art bottling machine.

equipment from Italy. In November 2006, two large semitrucks
delivered five thousand-gallon stainless-steel tanks, a new
crusher and press, and an automated bottling machine to the
winery. The equipment arrived only days before their big Nouveau Wine Release Party. "We bottled fourteen thousand bottles
of wine on the new machine in a day and a half to be ready for
the party," McFarland said.

Mac's Creek Winery grows Edelweiss, Marechal Foch, Brianna, De Chaunac, Saint Croix, LaCrosse, Frontenac, and Vignoles
grapes on site and buys grapes from ten other Nebraska growers. Max McFarland likes the Marechal Foch and Brianna varieties the best. He considers Brianna a cold-hardy and disease-
resistant vine. "Ed Swanson and I have the coldest vineyard
spots in Nebraska," he claimed. "One of our most difficult problems is that we often get a late spring frost. If bud break has
occurred before the frost, the vine usually won't produce any
fruit that year." McFarland is working with several universities
on a research project where they paint the buds by hand with

Mac's Creek wines, including Buzzard's Roost Blush, have won many awards.

a seaweed derivative to delay bud break up to ten days. "It's a very labor intensive process," he said. In cooperation with Ohio State University, he is also using a spray made from soybeans in another research project funded by a grant from the Nebraska Grape Board. The McFarlands use three different trellis systems and net the vines after the grapes mature to control bird damage. They use compost for fertilizer, employing few insecticides, and disinfect with water containing ozone. "We want to be good stewards of the land and conserve the resources of our community," McFarland said.

The local community has shown great interest and support for their new venture. "We get a lot of volunteer help, especially at harvest time, and the people in the community support our special events," Max McFarland said. Special events include a Soup du' Jour Dinner each Saturday in December and January, a Night of Wine and Roses for Valentine's Day in February, an Irish celebration dinner and concert in March, the Great Buzzard Migration Wine Release Party in May, a Father's Day Barbecue in June, a Night of New England Seafood in July, a Harvest Brunch in September, and the Nouveau Wine Release Party in November.

Of course the wine is what makes the celebration memorable. The McFarlands give their wines interesting names associated with family history or lore of Nebraska. Mac's Lantern, a red wine made from Frontenac grapes, recalls the McFarland family of Scotland, who were well known for cattle rustling under a full moon, referred to as "Mac's lantern." Bud's Reserve, another bold and smooth red from Frontenac grapes, honors the qualities of the winemaker's father, Dale ("Bud") McFarland. FJ's Reserve, a white wine from Seyval grapes, is named for F. Joseph O'Neill, Theresa McFarland's father. Buffalo Wallow, a semisweet white wine from Seyval grapes is named for the buffalo, "who paw the dry dirt of the prairie to make a wallow." Flatwater White is a sweet white wine from Edelweiss and LaCrosse grapes, named for the Otoe Indian word *nebraska*, which means "flat water." River Valley Red, a sweet red wine, is named for the location of Mac's Creek vineyards in the Platte River Valley. Buzzard's Roost Blush, which combines the essences of strawberry, grapefruit, lemon, and lime, is named for buzzards that frequent a local canyon.

The legend of Buzzard's Roost is one of Max McFarland's favorite family stories. According to McFarland's uncle, Jesse James hid his treasures in a canyon near Lexington, Nebraska, where the buzzards always flew backwards to stick their tail feathers into the clay banks to roost for the evening. The Great Buzzard Migration Wine Release Party, one of the most popular events at Mac's Creek Winery, is held each May when buzzards really do roost in the canyons north of the vineyard. Buzzard's Roost Blush often sells out rapidly. When customers beg for more, Max McFarland tells them that there will be no more until the "buzzards come to roost again next spring."

LAND OF THE PIONEERS

Bohemian Alps Vineyard Brainard, Nebraska

In the spring, the Bohemian Alps spread themselves out like a carpet woven with every possible shade of green. To Czech and German immigrants, the rolling hills of this part of Nebraska reminded them of their homeland, and they named the area the Bohemian Alps. From a hilltop at the Bruce and Jan Bostelman farm, the viewer can trace the pattern of hues ranging from the forest green of oak and black walnut trees, the emerald green of pristine prairie grass, the sea green of pasture, the mint green of newly sprouted corn, and the apple green of rows of grape-vines. The Bostelman's three-acre Bohemian Alps Vineyard is located next to pasture and virgin prairie grass sprinkled with native wildflowers. Dedicated to promoting diversified agricul-tural practices on small farms, the Bostelmans also grow and sell products to wholesale floral companies and provide tours for visitors of all ages.

Bruce Bostelman, a retired military man, is on his second career as vintner and horticulturist for the farm. "When I was stationed in the air force in Omaha, I got to know the folks at James Arthur Vineyards and decided that when I retired I'd buy a farm somewhere in Nebraska and raise grapes," he said. The couple and their son soon found themselves owning their one hundred sixty-acre farm, where they all tend the De Chaunac, Frontenac, Saint Croix, Traminette, and LaCrosse grapevines. From the hilltop vineyard, they can survey the tallgrass prairie where flocks of wild turkeys and deer roam the nearby slopes. Jan Bostelman does her share of vineyard work, but she enjoys photographing the plants and has won many awards for her work. "I just love to see changes in the vines through all phases of growth and development," she said.

The Bostelman's dog and a few rows of smooth wire around the perimeter of the vineyard help discourage deer from munch-ing the tender grape leaves. "It's not fun to put netting on the

The Bohemian Alps Vineyard is set amid the rolling hills of southeastern Nebraska near Brainard.

vines, but we have to do it to protect the maturing grapes from the birds," Bostelman said. He likes the Frontenac vines the best. "They seem to do well in our clay and loam soil, they like the cold weather, and they produce well, giving us about ten pounds of grapes to each vine," he said. Other vineyard management practices include using vertical shoot positioning on a high-wire trellis system for training the vines, the minimal use of fertilizer and insect spray, and good canopy management. "You have to get in there and pull out leaves when they start to get too thick. The fruit needs just the right amount of shade and sunshine to produce quality grapes," he added. Friends, family, and local

The high-wire trellis system is visible behind owners Jan and
Bruce Bostelman, who stand among the rows of their vineyard.

high-school students help during the late summer and early fall
grape harvest. The grapes are transported to Four Winds Vineyard near Ashland, Nebraska, to be processed into wine.

Visitors to the vineyard are encouraged to attend events in
the surrounding area, where "the Czech farm families cook up
wonderful cultural foods like roasted duck, kraut, and dumplings.
You can travel to the many small towns and church parishes
and get a good meal every weekend in the summer," Jan Bostelman said. One mile from the vineyard is a thirteen-mile-long
crushed-white-rock walking and biking trail running between
Brainard and Valparaiso through high plains to wooded areas
and bridges. Southwest of the vineyard, near Dwight, is the
home of the former poet laureate of the United States, Ted
Kooser. Of the Bohemian Alps, Kooser wrote in his book *Local
Wonders*, they "run about forty miles north and south and five
or six miles east and west. No more than a hundred feet from
bottom to top, they're made up of silty clay and gravelly glacial
till with small red boulders that look like uncooked pot roasts."

Grapevines frame the vineyard farmstead in an
idyllic scene in the Bohemian Alps of Nebraska.

Whether you choose a hearty Czech meal in one of the dozens of
small towns dotting the rolling hillsides or a stroll through the
grapevines, prairie grass, and woody florals, the Bohemian Alps
offer a feast for your stomach, eyes, and soul.

Whiskey Run Creek Vineyard and Winery

Brownville, Nebraska

Whiskey Run Creek Vineyard and Winery is located near the end of Main Street in the historic village of Brownville, only a stone's throw from the Missouri River. Settled in 1854, the town became a major steamboat landing, river crossing, overland freighting terminus, and milling center. Many of the early buildings have been restored, including a one-hundred-year-old barn that serves as the winery's tasting room. Robert E. Curttright, the winery's founder, had the historic structure moved eighteen miles to its current location spanning Whiskey Run Creek. The barn, built near the turn of the nineteenth century, is held together by wooden pegs instead of nails. On the property, Curttright also restored the caves of an old brewery built around 1866. The caves had been filled with dirt, probably during Prohibition. The brewery building was long gone, and the site was covered with vegetation. Curttright thought people might appreciate seeing the beautiful, all-brick architecture of the caves. Excavated and renovated, they now house wine barrels and are included on a tour of Whiskey Run Creek.

After a career as a businessman, Curttright retired to the Brownville area and purchased 122 acres of farmland that had once belonged to his grandparents. In 1998, staff members from the University of Nebraska planted grapes in a test plot on the land, and Curttright planted more vines in 1999. The concept of starting a winery became a passion with Curttright, and he put his time and effort into developing Whiskey Run Creek despite repeated medical tests that indicated he had cancer. Even when his health deteriorated, he would visit the facility and greet customers and friends. Curttright died on 22 June 2007, and his family placed the vineyard and winery up for sale.

Ron Heskett, the winemaker at Whiskey Run Creek, also grows seven acres of vines for the winery. Heskett said he was

A brick-lined cave was part of a brewery that once operated at the site of Whiskey Run Creek Winery in Brownville. The cave now houses wine barrels and offers an appealing locale for intimate dinners.

looking at alternative crops for his grain and cow/calf operation when he decided to plant a few grapevines. He did some reading and took a wine course as preparation. All of the Whiskey Run Creek wines are his favorites because, he said, "I'm the wine-maker!" He runs the winery largely by himself since Curttright's death, but he has some part-time help at harvest. Whiskey Run Creek wines include their Riesling, a delicate white wine made from Nebraska's only Riesling grape; Concord, a sweet dessert wine that pairs well with chocolate; and Frontenac, a medium-dry red wine produced from the best-known and most reliable

Winemaker Ron Heskett pours wine in the restored barn
at Whiskey Run Creek Winery.

Stainless-steel tanks hold fermenting wine in the
modern production facility at Whiskey Run Creek.

Visitors to this former barn that now serves as the tasting room at Whiskey Run Creek can watch the stream flow underneath them.

grapes for vintners in the high plains states. The winery also makes several fruit wines, including honey-raspberry, apple-raspberry, honey-apple, and honey-blackberry.

The winery hosts dinners and private parties, and a wedding is held on-site about once a month. Heskett's daughter leads tours through the winery, production facility, and historic caves, which a writer for the *Lincoln Journal-Star* described as "a secret-feeling, stone-walled, intriguing space." Visitors can also sit in the tasting room in the old barn, sip wine, and watch the peaceful creek flow underneath them. Just down the street, visitors will find the Captain Meriwether Lewis Steamboat Museum, a number of historic houses, seven art galleries, two restaurants, and many shops in the town of Brownville, Nebraska, which is a National Historic District. A stop at Whiskey Run Creek Vineyard and Winery could thus top off an exploration of places with a past.

SchillingBridge Winery and Microbrewery
Pawnee City, Nebraska

Colorful history is woven into the location of SchillingBridge Winery and MicroBrewery near Pawnee City, Nebraska, where owners Mike and Sharon Schilling share a passion for preserving the past and moving into the future. "The tranquil countryside on the west edge of Pawnee City provides a destination site that bridges the gap between our vineyard's past history while encompassing innovative ideas for our exciting future," the Schillings said. The owners' enthusiasm shines through as they guide visitors around the sparkling new winery and immaculate vineyards. "People need to step up and stop losing rural America," Mike Schilling added. "We know people can do great things and make sacrifices for the next generation. That's part of what we are trying to do at SchillingBridge Winery."

With a strong agricultural business background—they owned and operated grain elevators and fertilizer and chemical businesses—the Schillings brought knowledge and experience into their new venture. "When we bought this property, Mike said we ought to plant a few grapes. I thought maybe we'd plant one hundred fifty vines; we planted fifteen hundred," Sharon Schilling explained. The vineyard now covers more than eight acres and encompasses two unique attractions: an 1890s limestone Rock Island Railroad bridge and the site where staff from the University of Nebraska excavated the burial of two Asian elephants that are currently on display in Lincoln. Visitors can stroll on a gravel pathway near the excavation site, through the vineyard, and on down to the historic bridge that inspired the winery's name. Several SchillingBridge wines honor the railroad history of Pawnee City. Burlington is a classic white wine from Seyval Blanc grapes aged in oak; Rock Island Red is a full-bodied red wine made from the Chambourcin grape; and Right

An 1890s limestone railroad bridge is the historic site for which SchillingBridge Winery near Pawnee City, Nebraska, is named.

O'Way is a light red wine crafted to be enjoyed sooner rather than later.

The label of Forever Venus, the signature wine of Schilling-Bridge, tells the story of how the elephants, named Venus and Hamburg, came to be buried beside the old railroad line. Traveling the Rock Island Railroad, the Campbell Brothers Circus arrived at the site in May 1904. The dropping of an open torch caused a fire in which the elephants died. They were then buried "forty paces past the 'whistling post.'" In 1906, the skeletons were excavated and displayed at Morrill Hall at the University of Nebraska in Lincoln. Several other circus animals were also killed in the fire and are still buried in a mound near the old railroad line, according to Sharon Schilling. The "whistling post" is the spot where the railroad engineer was required to blow his whistle to let the townspeople know the train was arriving. The label for Forever Venus displays a picture of a mother elephant and her baby. A painting of the pair also hangs near the fireplace in the winery tasting room. "Venus was actually known as

Another historic site on the winery property is the whistling post
on the route of the historic Rock Island Railroad.

a killer elephant in the circus, and Hamburg was not even her
baby, but it was said that Venus lovingly cared for the younger
elephant," Schilling explained.

A walk through the vineyard on sloping hillsides leads the
visitor down to the creek and the old railroad bridge through
well-groomed rows of vines. The varieties include Aurora,
Seyval Blanc, LaCrosse, Traminette, De Chaunac, Chambourcin,
Marquis, Venus Table Grape, and Baco Noir. Vintners need to
understand their own unique microclimates to determine what
grapes and management practices will work best in their vineyards. The vintners in southeastern Nebraska, where the climate is slightly less harsh, are able to grow some grape varieties
that most vintners on the high plains cannot. As she guides visitors around the vineyard, Sharon Schilling lovingly tucks stray
vines through trellis wires to keep them growing toward the
sky. "It's a constant job to keep the vines pruned and trained to
the trellis," she explained. The Schillings' management program
includes fertilizers and chemicals, as determined by laboratory
tests, for controlling growth, disease, and pests. To keep deer

Sharon Schilling tucks a vine back into place in the SchillingBridge vineyard.

out of the vineyard, they hang a mesh bag containing a specific brand of soap at the end of each row. "It works; don't buy the cheap soap, though," Sharon Schilling said.

In winemaking, the Schillings consider a good laboratory an important component. "The lab is your lifeline for making a good product," Mike Schilling said. The Schillings have employed Max Hoffman as their winemaker. "Max had grown up around here, raised Nebraska crops for more than thirty years, and operated a hog farm. We call him our swine to wine person," Schilling said. The production area of the winery includes a crusher and press, along with several polyvinyl tanks for fermentation and a machine that fills and caps one thousand bottles per hour. Some of the wine is aged in oak barrels.

Sharon and Mike Schilling stand in front of the
"wall of wine" at their winery near Pawnee City.

The Schillings have depended on the experience of others
in building their business. "Just because you grow something
doesn't mean you can make a unique product from it that
people will want," Mike Schilling said. One of the people who
have been influential is Ed Swanson of Cuthills Vineyard. "Ed
is a genius and has been very important in the growth of the
wine industry in Nebraska. If he likes and respects you, he'll
spend time with you," Schilling added. The Schillings are proud
of their children, Kelly, Dallas, and Jonathan. "Our dream is for
them to carry the business forward, but we encourage them to
discover their own dreams," Sharon said. SchillingBridge Winery opened on 26 November 2005, with an event attended by
Nebraska governor Dave Heineman and a thousand other visitors. "We were so excited, proud, and happy," Sharon Schilling
said. "We want the local people to be proud of our community
and our contribution."

The winery includes a banquet room for private parties and

public events. Two of the most popular activities include "Murder at SchillingBridge," an interactive murder mystery dinner theater, and a comedy festival named Laughter and Libations. On 25 May 2007, Sharon Schilling hosted a new event for the release of a new wine called Women Gone Wine. "We had one hundred forty women here who enjoyed a wine and dessert bar and entertainment by comedian Marni Vos. It was a great night for the women," Schilling said. Women Gone Wine is a blush table wine described on the label as "a sassy fruit-forward wine that has been handcrafted with today's playful woman in mind. Its berry flavors ripple with sweet seduction—yet invite savvy women to unite for an evening of high spiritedness and fun."

On the "wall of wine" in the tasting room, visitors can view wines ranging from white to blush to red. The winery has garnered many awards, including double-gold and best-of-show white wine at the Florida State International Wine Competition for its 2006 Edelweiss. The label for the Edelweiss expresses the Schillings' vision for the winery. "SchillingBridge Winery and MicroBrewery is bridging the gap between the wine connoisseur and the beer enthusiast," the label reads. In the future, the Schillings hope to expand the microbrewery, add a historical train, and build a bed and breakfast. "It's like *Field of Dreams*," Mike Schilling said. "Build it and they will come." The Schillings are also avid promoters of Pawnee City, a small town with fifty-six properties on the National Registry of Historic Places. It is named for the Pawnee Indians who once lived among the gently rolling hills, and the area remains a hunter's paradise with deer, wild turkey, pheasant, and quail in abundance. People in Pawnee City enjoy a quality of life that few small towns offer, and SchillingBridge is a contributing factor.

METRO REGION

Soaring Wings Vineyard Springfield, Nebraska

Former military and commercial pilot Jim Shaw and his wife, Sharon, owners of Soaring Wings Vineyard, say that their foray into the winemaking business was exactly like "jumping off the proverbial cliff." Even so, Shaw's winemaking career began when he was only thirteen years old. He shared a batch of clandestinely made mulberry wine with some buddies in south Omaha. "My mother quickly cured me of this endeavor, though, when she found five gallons of apple wine fermenting in my closet," Jim Shaw admitted. Although he made his first few dollars selling wine to his teenage friends, it would be more than thirty years before he was ready to jump back into making and selling wine.

The Shaws searched for a year to find the perfect location for their vineyard. They purchased several acres on one of the highest spots in Sarpy County near the farming community of Springfield, Nebraska. "I chose it for its location close to the Omaha market, its spectacular view, and its potential to provide an entertainment venue to go along with the vineyard and winery," Shaw said. The couple also struggled to find an appropriate name for the vineyard. Because Jim had received silver wings as an air force pilot, they considered the name Silver Wings, but they found that a prominent European winemaker already claimed that name. They decided on Soaring Wings and discovered they liked it better, anyway. In 2002, they planted the first vines on five acres. "There were still dead cornstalks in the field where we planted twenty-five hundred vines," Sharon Shaw said. "I was stumbling over the stubs of old stalks, mumbling and crying and yelling at Jim, 'what are we doing?' We had family helping us plant. . . . At the end of the job, they told us 'don't ever call us again.'"

After attending numerous seminars, conducting research, and completing an advanced winemaking course from the Uni-

A row of grapevines leads visitors to the Soaring Wings
winery near Springfield, Nebraska.

versity of California at Davis, the Shaws opened their winery
in August 2003. Jim Shaw is the head winemaker and oversees
the vineyard, construction, and business plans. Sharon Shaw
manages the tasting room and public events. They also receive
assistance from their children, Jeremy, Sara, and Teresa. The
winemaking facility began modestly with a crusher, press, and
a few fermenting tanks. The primary fermenting tank was an

Winemaker and owner Jim Shaw points out the barrels used to age many wines at Soaring Wings.

old dairy tank that had been used on the farm in Iowa where Sharon grew up. "My Dad was very happy and proud to be able to taste the first wine made in his old dairy tank. Funny thing, Dad never drank before, but he liked our wine," Sharon Shaw said.

By 2007, the business had grown to eight acres of grapevines and had contracts with ten other growers to produce grapes for the winery. They hired two full-time employees—one works in the tasting room and handles distribution to area markets and vendors, while the other works in the vineyard and assists in winemaking and bottling. They had also added several large stainless-steel tanks, oak barrels, and a bottling machine to the production facility. The vineyard contains Vignoles, Frontenac, LaCrosse, De Chaunac, Chardonel, Chambourcin, and Tramanette vines. Shaw irrigates to get the vines started but finds that it is not necessary to do so most of the time. He controls the birds by hanging flashing silver objects, such as compact discs, throughout the vineyard and by using birdcalls. He applies some commercial fertilizer but prefers compost and uses minimal amounts of insect spray. Shaw's favorite vine is the Frontenac because, he says, "it is disease and cold resistant, and it makes a good wine."

In the production facility, Shaw aspires to "make excellent Nebraska wine that will be well-known across the land as quality wine." He uses an ozone sterilization machine to clean the equipment, filters all wines, and ages many in oak barrels. The wines of Soaring Wings have won more than eighty awards in almost four years of competition. Dragon's Red, a semisweet red wine made from Frontenac grapes with fruity notes and a bit of bite, was named the 2007 best red hybrid in the region east

Sharon and Jim Shaw greet visitors in the tasting room of
Soaring Wings Vineyard, with many of their award-winning
vintages on display.

of the West Coast. Winter White, similar to a Riesling and made
from LaCrosse grapes, was listed for three years in the top fifty
wines east of the West Coast. Moonstruck, a white wine with
hints of pear, apple, and pineapple, has won many international
competitions. Other labels include Vignoles, a sweet white
made from Vignoles grapes; Soaring Eagle, a semidry red wine
from a blend of grapes; and Ice Falcon, a semisweet white wine
blended from Vignoles, Chardonel, and LaCrosse grapes.

Visitors to Soaring Wings Vineyards can purchase an assort-
ment of Nebraska cheeses, meats, bread, and chocolates to
accompany the vintages. Customers may enjoy a wine tasting
inside the Tuscan-accented tasting room, or they may choose to
sit outside with a basket of food and wine and take in the view.
The winery sits at the top of a hill with a gentle slope leading
to the vineyards and an event stage. Ample parking accommo-
dates visitors, who sit on the grassy hillside to view the many
performances offered throughout the season. The annual Wine

and Blues Festival in May kicks off the summer activities with national touring acts as well as local bands. The Nebraska Balloon Club launches hot air balloons in the evening and food is available. On Friday evenings during the summer, local jazz or acoustic bands are on stage. Visitors are encouraged to bring lawn chairs and a picnic.

During harvest season, guests can attend an old-fashioned pig roast in an event called Swine-on-the-Vine. Reservations are required. The Harvest Festival in September celebrates the end of the season with grape stomping, live music, and food and wine. The winter months are filled with meet-your-winemaker dinners and barrel tastings. Reservations are required for these special events. The Shaws also offer tours, private parties, receptions, weddings, and team-building and fund-raising events. From high on a hilltop in Nebraska, the sky is the limit at Soaring Wings.

Prime Country Winery Denton, Nebraska

At Prime Country Winery, row upon row of grapevines march across the verdant hillsides like drummers in a band showing off their best formations. From a hilltop near the center of the vineyard, one can see the Denton Hills area, once part of the tallgrass prairie. Orville Gertsch, the seventy-eight-year-old patriarch of the winery, grew up on a Nebraska farm not far away. He moved to California as a young adult, married, and became an electrician and general contractor. "I came back to Nebraska every fall to go hunting. On one trip I decided to buy a farm. I kept buying and selling farms; then, fourteen farms later, I ended up with this one where we planted the grapes and started the winery," he said.

Gertsch has always marched to his own drummer. A Nebraska farm family who had emigrated from Switzerland raised him after his mother died and his father left. They were kind to him, but he was often alone. He would go off fishing on his own, carrying a sack containing a frying pan, flour, and lard. "I'd catch me a nice mess of bluegills, clean them, fry them, and have me a little feast," he recalled. "I'd seen lots of wild grapes growing along the Platte River when I was hunting and fishing. So, I thought, if wild grapes can grow here, I should be able to raise them." On his return to Nebraska, Gertsch visited some nurseries and did some research. An advertisement in a magazine from a local winery looking for Nebraska grape growers convinced him that a vineyard could be a paying proposition.

With the help of his son Fred, who also moved to Nebraska from California, Gertsch began planning the vineyard. In 1998, the two men planted six acres of vines and added new plantings nearly every year. The vineyard now covers twenty acres with several varieties of American and French vines. For two years, the Gertschs sold some of their harvest to a winery that advertised for grapes. Eventually they converted an old machine

Rows of grapevines march across the hillside at
Prime Country Winery near Denton, Nebraska.

Winemaker and owner Orville Gertsch pours wine in the tasting room of Prime Country Winery.

shed into a production facility and tasting room and opened their own winery in 2002. "Everyone said I couldn't raise grapes here or make wine, but I was sure that I could. I say I'm determined; my wife says I'm stubborn," Gertsch said. His wife, Dorothy, helps out in the tasting room at the winery. "She raised four kids and she's put up with me for fifty-three years, so I'd say she's a wonderful woman."

Before becoming a vintner, Orville Gertsch read many books, attended several University of Nebraska workshops and seminars, and received support and help from Ed Swanson of Cuthills Vineyard. Somewhat of a maverick, though, Gertsch says, "I do things my way." Specifically, the Gertschs do not irrigate their grapes and use no chemicals in the vineyard. "Everything is done by manual labor from planting to pruning through harvest," Orville Gertsch explained. "I believe that proper air movement through the vineyard and proper pruning of the grapes, along with keeping the vineyard scrupulously clean, keeps the vineyard disease and pest free," he added.

Gertsch has been making wine as a hobby for more than thirty years and professionally for six years. "In our first year of operation, we did not bottle any wine until it was at least eighteen months old; since that time we do not bottle any wine until it is at least twenty-four months old," he said. Once the wine is fermented, he does not pump the wine for racking. Instead, the sediment is siphoned off into clean containers several times by gravity and the wine is filtered before bottling. Gertsch ferments the wine in polyvinyl vats and stainless-steel tanks and uses no oak barrels for aging. At harvest, the grapes are all hand-picked into five-gallon food-grade plastic buckets, then brought to the winery for crushing and pressing. Any water used during

These and other wines are available at Prime Country Winery.

grape processing is used to water trees around the property, and grape stems are fed to cattle. Prime Country hires some part-time vineyard help during pruning and harvesting seasons, but the winery is run completely by the family.

Prime Country Winery currently produces about fifteen hundred gallons a year, or approximately eight thousand bottles of wine. All wine is sold at the winery. The list includes several red and white wines made from two or three combinations of grape varieties, including Edelweiss, De Chaunac, Saint Vincent, Saint Croix, Concord, Swenson Red, Frontenac, Niagara, Brianna, and Prairie Star. "I was told I couldn't make good wine from Concord grapes," Gertsch said. "But, I've had many customers who rave over my Concord grape wine. And, I've even had people from California, including a vintner, buy the Concord wine." Other favorite wines and bestsellers include Lancaster White and Lancaster Red, both named for Lancaster County where Prime Country Winery is located. On 4 May 2007, a tornado struck the Prime Country vineyard, stripping the leaves from hundreds of grapevines and pushing many vines to the ground. "We lost a lot of production for the year," Gertsch said, "But, we'll carry on just like we always do."

Lancaster County includes several small towns as well as the city of Lincoln, home of the Nebraska state capitol and the University of Nebraska. Three miles west of Prime Country Winery is Spring Creek Prairie, a six-hundred-forty-acre site featuring miles of walking trails through the tallgrass prairie, wetlands, and riparian woodlands. The miles and miles of rolling hillsides surrounding Prime Country Winery provide a peaceful setting for a family outing. The owners do not plan any specific public events but will host group events and tours on request. At Prime Country Winery, the grapevines continue to march across the heart of the Nebraska grasslands, while the owner steps to the beat of his own drum.

Deer Springs Winery Lincoln, Nebraska

The spirit of Irish immigrant Patrick O'Halloran lives on at the homestead he founded in 1868 on the outskirts of Lincoln, Nebraska. His friendly spirit seems to pop in now and then to see if his great-great granddaughters are taking proper care of his heritage. Kathleen Hennigar and Jennifer Reeder are proud of their great-great grandfather and established the tasting room for their family business, Deer Springs Winery, in Patrick O'Halloran's original house. The wall of the remodeled building displays a copy of the deed to the property, signed in 1874 by President Ulysses S. Grant.

Hennigar and Reeder grew up in California, where their father, Jim Partington, was a navy pilot. Partington retired in 1992 and moved back to Nebraska with his wife, Barbara. He had spent his childhood summers working on the farm for his great-uncle, the second Patrick O'Halloran, and eventually inherited the property. Hennigar and Reeder also moved back to the state. "We'd always loved the small vineyards and wineries around Paso Robles, California," Reeder said. "We started thinking of how we could use the old homestead and buildings in a way that we could share with other people." A small portion of the Oregon Trail crosses one corner of the property, and the women wanted to preserve that history, too.

"Dad worked really hard to fix up the property after it had been neglected for years. He had to clean up old wire and fence posts and re-dig and stock the pond with fish," Hennigar said. "We all decided we should take advantage of our unique heritage and location, so we thought planting a vineyard would enhance the beauty of our land." They planted one acre of Edelweiss, LaCrosse, Bianca, Vignoles, Saint Croix, Saint Vincent, and Lemberger vines in 2001. The first harvest in 2004 was mostly sold to another winery, but they kept a few Bianca grapes to make wine. "It was quite a project. We crushed the grapes by

Homesteader Patrick O'Halloran once lived in this house, which is now the tasting room at Deer Springs Winery near Lincoln.

hand, and it took all day long to get enough juice to fill a three-gallon carboy jug," Reeder said. "We served the wine at Christmas and were amazed at how good it tasted," said Hennigar. She convinced her sister to use her scientific knowledge to become a winemaker.

The entire family (consisting of Jim and Barbara Partington; Kathleen Hennigar and son John; Jennifer Reeder and husband, Jon, and twins Aislinn and Ryan) found themselves forming a family business and picking out a name for a winery. Their first choice, Homestead Winery, was already trademarked, and it took a while to find another name that everyone liked. "One misty spring evening as Jennifer and I sat on the patio, a herd of deer walked through the meadow by the spring-fed pond. Behind them appeared the most beautiful rainbow," Barbara Partington said. "Jennifer and I both exclaimed, 'Deer Springs,' and we'd found the name for our winery."

The entire family helped plant more grapevines and repair the surviving buildings. The old granary was turned into the production facility, and the original house was remodeled for the tasting room. "I didn't really want to keep the old house at first, but then I decided it would be a really good idea to honor great-great grandfather Patrick by sharing his house with visitors," Reeder recalled. The old immigrant must have agreed

Sisters Kathleen Hennigar, left, and Jennifer Reeder stand
next to one of the carboy glass containers they use to process
wine at Deer Springs Winery near Lincoln, Nebraska.

because he seemingly appeared one day when Hennigar was
reading in the house. "I looked up from my book and saw the
hazy image of a farmer dressed in overalls and an old hat standing in the corner smiling," she said. "I was shocked and looked
back down at my book. When I glanced back up, he was gone.
I'm sure it was Patrick O'Halloran. He seemed friendly and I
didn't feel scared. I think he was giving us his blessing."

Deer Springs Winery opened in late summer 2007. By then
the sisters had three hundred grapevines and planned to supplement the crop with grapes bought from other growers. Reeder
resigned from her teaching job to work full-time in the winery.
Hennigar still teaches school, and Jim Partington is the director
of the Nebraska Restaurant Association. Each family member

The modern-day production facility at Deer Springs Winery
began life as a farm granary.

does the work she or he loves best in the vineyard and winery.
"Jennifer loves the grapes, she has endless patience and treats
the vines like they are her babies, so she is the winemaker.
Kathleen likes to talk to people, so she is the tasting-room manager. The grandkids help out wherever needed, and I take care
of the business affairs," Barbara Partington explained. Everyone
works in the vineyard during pruning and harvesting season.

The vines are trained on a two-wire cordon trellis except
for the Bianca vines, which grow on a vertical-shoot-position
trellis. Management practices include the use of some fertilizer and insect spray and netting to control the birds. Reeder is
most fond of the Bianca grapes, which were developed in Hun-
gary, and the wine they produce. "There's something about the
unique floral quality of the Bianca wine," she said. She plans
to make Bianca the signature wine of Deer Springs Winery.
Present wines include Firefly White, a blend of LaCrosse and
Edelweiss grapes; Prairie Sunset, a blend of red grapes; Prairie

Sunrise, a blend of white grapes; and Gypsy Red, made from Lemberger grapes.

"The location of the vineyard and winery is near perfect," Barbara Partington said. "We are a few minutes from Lincoln and an hour from Omaha. We're close enough to town and yet we still have a country feel. We want to keep our facility small with a real farm winery atmosphere," she added. Deer Springs Winery hosts small, intimate events with a casual atmosphere. If great-great grandfather Patrick O'Halloran wants to drop by, he is welcome to try the wine, too.

James Arthur Vineyards Raymond, Nebraska

Each May, Nebraska's largest vineyard and winery celebrates the elements of renewal, rebirth, and the revival of art and learning with a Renaissance Festival. The concept of renaissance perfectly describes the accomplishments at James Arthur Vineyard since it opened in 1997. Grapes once grew prolifically in Nebraska. Before Prohibition in 1920, nearly fifty thousand grapevines were growing in the state. When it became illegal to make or sell alcoholic beverages, the vines went out of production, and other crops replaced grapes. The vineyards waited decades before their renaissance late in the twentieth century.

James Arthur Vineyards started as a "hobby gone wild," said winemaker Jim Ballard. His father-in-law, Jim Jeffers, owned farmland that contained rolling hills with rocky, sandy soil and south-facing slopes with good drainage. Brisk winds kept out pests, and the land provided all the ingredients for growing grapes. Ballard planted several grapevines and hoped his hobby would produce enough homemade wine to share with family and friends. Today, his wines are being shared with thousands of visitors from every state and forty-seven foreign countries. "Visitors are usually amazed that we can really grow grapes in Nebraska," Ballard said. "We encourage people to relax and enjoy their visit to our winery. If people come with an open mind, they'll really appreciate our wines. We're not California or New York; our wines should be enjoyed for what they are—a real taste of Nebraska."

The vineyards, set on four hundred acres of rolling hills and natural prairie grasslands, offer a picturesque setting in which visitors can try the wines, stroll the grounds, relax under hilltop gazebos, and tour the farm and production facility. "People are our priority," Ballard said. He has learned that most people love to hear stories and experience the place firsthand. "They like to touch the green leaves on the vines. They like to touch the cold,

smooth surface of the fermenting tanks, and they like to feel the
warm wood texture of the oak barrels." Visitors also like to meet the
owners and staff of James Arthur
Vineyards and discover the history
of the facility, which started when
Jim and Neenie Jeffers purchased a
few hundred acres near Raymond,
Nebraska, in 1992. Jim Jeffers had
owned a deli-meat manufacturing
plant in Omaha, and they planned
to retire and spend time with their
children and grandchildren. When
son-in-law Jim Ballard's hobby
got out of hand, however, Jeffers
was only too happy to jump back

Winemaker Jim Ballard
pours one of his award-
winning vintages in the
tasting room of James
Arthur Vineyards near
Raymond, Nebraska.

into business. Eventually the family founded the vineyard and
named it James Arthur Vineyards (JAV) using Jim Jeffers's first
and middle names, James Arthur. The family considers the winery to be their gift to Nebraskans and to the people who visit
the Cornhusker state.

The Jeffers's daughter, Barb Ballard, and her husband Jim
soon became immersed in the day-to-day operation of the vineyard and winery. The winery employs a tasting-room manager,
a vineyard manager, and other local people, including a director of sales and distribution. The little vineyard that began as
a hobby with two hundred fifty vines has grown to more than
nine thousand vines. JAV also contracts with twenty-three area
grape growers for their grapes. "Grapevines love Nebraska soil,"
Jim Ballard said. French-American hybrids, including Saint
Croix, LaCrosse, Edelweiss, Vignoles, and Frontenac, are the
mainstays of the vineyard. Their most popular and bestselling
wine is made from the Edelweiss white grape. "Edelweiss has
put Nebraska on the map, as far as wines go," Ballard said. "I
truly believe our sweet white wines can compete against any-

An artificial owl guards the James Arthur vines, attempting to frighten birds away from the ripening grapes.

one in the world." The James Arthur Edelweiss has won numerous medals in competitions, both national and international.

Ballard contends that producing good wines "begins in the vineyard." His management practices are basic: choosing the right trellis system for each vine, constant mowing and weeding, and good canopy management. "We use very few chemicals or fertilizer," he explained. To keep the birds at bay, they use birdcalls, Mylar balloons, pie pans, or anything that reflects the light. "We also walk or ride through the vineyard constantly to discourage birds and other wildlife. It is not practical to use netting on twenty acres of vines, so we don't usually net the vines except for a few late harvest grapes," he added. "We are constantly testing the soil and the plants to monitor their nutritional needs." The vineyard's soil is mostly clay and loam with natural prairie grass providing ground cover between the vineyard rows. Thousands of years ago, glacial movement formed the area, and the fields also contain many different sizes and types of stone. Some have been used to make waterfalls and goldfish ponds near the decks and seating areas outside the tasting room at the winery. Completed in 2002, this addition provides a meeting and party room overlooking both the Saint Croix grapevines outside and the wine production area inside. Beneath the meeting room is a barrel storage cellar where some of the wines are aged in oak.

The production facility contains sixteen stainless-steel tanks that each hold fifteen hundred to twenty-five hundred gallons for fermentation. There are also three thirty-five-hundred-gallon fermentation tanks. "Fermentation is a hands-on process," Ballard said. "Mother Nature predicts a lot that happens. We can control the sweetness by measuring the sugar content. We stop the fermentation when we believe the wine is ready, then we filter the wine four or five times before bottling." A machine fills and labels several thousand bottles a day. Production in 2006 totaled about twenty-eight thousand gallons, or one hundred thirty thousand bottles of wine. Labels include Game Bird Red, a mellow red wine made from Saint Vincent grapes, and Game

Wine bottles are filled and then passed along to be
corked and labeled in the James Arthur production facility.

Picnic tables await visitors at the picturesque winery and tasting room of James Arthur Vineyards.

Bird White, a semidry white wine; both are part of the JAV Game Bird Series. Nebraska White is a sweet wine made from LaCrosse grapes and packaged in a crimson bottle, the official team color of the University of Nebraska football team. Edyn's Blush, from a blend of LaCrosse and Concord grapes, is named for the winemaker's daughter. Similarly, 2 Brothers, from Edelweiss grapes, is named for the winemaker's two sons. *Amo Té* is a semisweet blush wine made from De Chaunac and Saint Pepin grapes. As youngsters, Jim and Neenie Jeffers exchanged love notes signed "*amo té* (Latin for "I Love You").

In addition to the Renaissance Festival held each May, JAV also hosts live music concerts every Saturday in June, July, and

August, plays, dinners, and a September harvest festival. Barb Ballard leads tour groups, pours wine, and carries boxes of wine to customers' cars. She is also an ambassador for the surrounding area. The winery is located only minutes from downtown Lincoln and an hour from Omaha. She often urges customers to visit nearby attractions, including the Museum of Nebraska History, the Great Plains Art Museum, and the International Quilt Study Center. A visit to James Arthur Vineyards is like a day in paradise. Bird trills echo off the rolling hills, waterfalls slide gently over rocks, and the wind whispers a love song—it is a place where visitors can begin their own renaissance.

LEWIS AND CLARK LAND

Nissen Winery Bow Valley, Nebraska

Bow Valley in northeastern Nebraska has been a pleasant place to live or to pass through for centuries. From American Indian hunters to explorers Meriwether Lewis and William Clark, pioneer settlers, and present day sojourners, the valley has provided a bountiful supply of sustenance for body and soul. The Nebraska Department of Tourism dubbed this area of Nebraska "Lewis and Clark Land." William Clark himself mentioned the area on 26 August 1804. "The river [is] verry full of Sand bars and Wide," he said, and the expedition "geathered great quantities of Grapes & three Kinds of Plumbs." To this same valley in the 1870s came the farming forebears of brothers Tim and David Nissen. Today, the brothers carry on the heritage of their German ancestors in Bow Valley and search for ways to revitalize their farm. Poor market conditions and small livestock herds led the Nissens to seek alternative crops to sustain both their farm and the greater community.

Tim Nissen had stayed on the family farm after high school, while David Nissen managed a garden store for many years. In 2001, Tim purchased the farm established by his maternal great-grandfather in 1872. It is situated on rolling hills with rocky, calcium-rich soil. David also decided to move back to the farm to help raise livestock and crops such as oats, alfalfa, corn, rye, and turnips. The brothers also planted grapes and fruit trees as alternative crops. "With my degree in horticulture and some experience in growing, grafting, and breeding grapes, I thought it would be a great idea to plant grapes on the farm," David Nissen said.

"Many people may think it foolish to trade in a comfortable lifestyle for one of uncertainty and risk," Nissen continued. "For us the decision was centered on our community and our heritage. In the 1880s, our [paternal] great-grandparents left the region of Westphalia, Germany, to come to the United States for

Tim Nissen, center, and other workers place netting over the grapevines to discourage birds from eating the maturing grapes at Nissen Winery near Bow Valley. *Courtesy of Nissen Winery*

a better life. They eventually settled in the rolling hills of north-eastern Nebraska." Together, the immigrants built a church, school, businesses, roads, homes, and farms. "Our great-grand-father, using his skills and ingenuity, built a house out of the native stone. The rock was gathered from the fields, was blasted into square blocks, and then assembled into a house. The house is still inhabited today and is located a mile from the present vineyard. We hope our vineyard is a tribute to the work of our grandparents," David Nissen said. The one hundred twenty-five residents of Bow Valley have also continued to provide for the needs of the community, building the town's water and sewer system and paved roads. "We feel that with hard work and inge-nuity we can continue to make Bow Valley economically viable and a more dynamic place in which to live and work. With the addition of a winery to the community, we will be bringing more tourists to the area," Tim Nissen said.

Grow tubes protect and support new grapevines at Nissen Winery. *Courtesy of Nissen Winery*

Viticulture is also a good fit for area soils, which have many properties in common with the prime wine-growing regions of Germany. The pH of the calcium-rich soil is 7.5 to 8.3, which gives the wine a unique flavor. "In Germany, these soils would be highly prized, but here they are marginal soils for grain production. We realize that conventional agriculture is a dead end for our community and rural America. We know that we have to change our farming operation to focus on dollars per acre, not more acres," Tim Nissen said. The brothers planted eighteen varieties of grapes on thirteen acres, with five hundred fifty vines per acre. Some of the grape varieties included Frontenac, LaCrosse, Saint Pepin, Chancellor, Concord, and Brianna. They also planted three thousand plum and chokecherry trees. In 2007, they made their first wine, approximately four hundred cases. The Nissens hope to build a tasting room at the intersection of Nebraska Highways 12 and 57, a little north of Bow Valley, which will be more accessible to tourists.

Before launching their business, the Nissens consulted with other Nebraska vintners, spending many hours "helping and learning from" Ed and Holly Swanson of Cuthills Vineyards. The Swansons offered moral and technical assistance. Both brothers plan to continue working at outside jobs in nearby Hartington, Nebraska, until the vineyard and winery are established and bringing in additional income. They have also formed an alliance, named the Heartland Experience, with six other farm families and rural businesses to promote locally grown foods and develop agricultural tourism for the area. "Working together we will all benefit from one another's customer base and prove once again—just like our forefathers—that anything is possible with a dream, ingenuity, and working collectively towards our common goals," Tim Nissen said.

Cuthills Vineyards Pierce, Nebraska

Looking out over the prairie hills on a misty spring morning, the viewer might imagine he or she is overlooking a vineyard in Tuscany. Row upon row of grapevines come to life—the gray vines creeping up toward the sunrise with buds about to break into new, green life. Surprisingly, the vista is not in Italy but in northeastern Nebraska, the state's first modern-day vineyard and winery. Six thousand grapevines stretch their necks toward the sky on seven acres of rolling hills at Cuthills Vineyards, producing the fruit for wines that have won hundreds of awards in national and international competitions.

Often referred to as "the grandfather of Nebraska vineyards," co-owner and wine master Ed Swanson is a pioneer in the field. He has been planting and breeding grapes and making wine for about thirty years. He first planted four acres of grapes in 1985 and considered it a mistake because it was "so much work." Although his grapes froze, and he did not get a crop for three years, he determined "to do this, no matter what happens." He first planted several varieties that did not work in the climate of northeastern Nebraska. "Grapes are very specific to what they call home, and the climate varies so much I don't like to make any generalized statements about what grapes to plant," he said. Some of the grape varieties Swanson now grows include De Chaunac, Leon Millot, Marechal Foch, LaCrosse, Petite Amie, Chancellor, Vidal, Saint Croix, Saint Pepin, Reliance, Baco, and Frontenac. He also has hundreds of experimental varieties and a few new vines he developed himself.

When Swanson started growing grapes, he got some help from an enology specialist at Purdue University named Ellie Butz. She told him to call her at home if he had any questions and could not reach her at the university. "I got so wrapped up in my vineyard project and needed her advice," Swanson recalled, "so I called her home phone number one day. When

Near Pierce, the burgundy metal roof of Cuthills Vineyards,
Nebraska's first modern vineyard, is visible from the road.

she answered I heard pots clanging, and she asked me to wait a
minute while she took her turkey out of the oven. It was then I
realized it was Thanksgiving Day and maybe I should get a life.
Ellie laughed about it and answered my questions."

In addition to planting grapes and making wine, Swanson
helps new winegrowers through the Nebraska Wine and Grape
Growers Association. He also supported the enactment of the
Nebraska Farm Wineries Act of 1986, which increased the upper
limit of wine production to fifty thousand gallons per winery
per year and provided a special tax break for wines made from
a minimum of seventy-five percent Nebraska-grown produce.
In 1997, the state legislature passed a bill that allowed consumption on premises as well as intra- and interstate shipment of
Nebraska wines. Also in 1997, the University of Nebraska began
assisting winegrowers by establishing test sites for growing
grapes on a commercial basis under the direction of Paul Read.
Previously, they only encouraged vintners who grew grapes in
home gardens.

Even though Ed Swanson has served on the Nebraska Grape
and Wine Board, he would "rather not be on a board or involved
in the politics of the industry," he said. "I'd rather be grafting

Grapevines grow just outside the winery at Cuthills Vineyard.

and breeding grapes. Breeding grapes is like having six hundred children to rein in; I have to figure out their personalities; every year they change. But I have to produce and sell wine to make a living," he concluded. When breeding grapes, Swanson has had good luck crossing the wild grape *Vitis riparia* with domestic grapes. One of his recent favorites, and a gold-medal winner, has been wine produced from the grape he named Temparia, a cross between Tempranillo, a Spanish grape, and *Vitis riparia*. Wine from this grape won the 2007 Jefferson Cup Invitational competition in Kansas City. "I hadn't even entered the competition; I just took the wine for the judges to taste. One judge, Doug

Pioneer winemaker and grape grower Ed Swanson stands next to the membrane press he designed and built to extract grape juice.

Frost, liked it so well he entered it in the competition, and it took a gold medal," Swanson said.

In making wine, Swanson prefers to work with one-hundred-percent Nebraska grapes or other fruits. Some of his most popular labels are Reserve Red, made entirely from a new variety of grape bred by Swanson; Prairie Red and Willow Blush, both made from a blend of grapes; and Indulgence, made from red raspberries grown one-half mile from the vineyard. Cuthills Vineyards focuses on producing wines that pair well with food. Ed Swanson is a self-taught winemaker who traveled to Ohio, Pennsylvania, and New York to observe and learn from other vintners. He even built his own stainless-steel membrane press for releasing the juice from the grapes at a cost of about six thousand dollars. A similar factory-built press would cost around twenty thousand dollars. He produces five thousand gallons of wine each year, making what he calls a "fruity wine" and fermenting most of his vintage in steel tanks using a small amount of oak for aging. "When making wine, you should do what the vineyard tells you to do. The weather always affects the quality of the wine. So, each year I experiment with what the vineyard produces to make my wine," Swanson said.

Ed and his wife, Holly, established the present winery in 1994. It is housed in a remodeled barn that was constructed in 1920 by John Koeppe, a member of one of the original German immigrant families who founded Pierce in 1869. In addition to the production area, the winery includes a tasting room and gift shop. From the outside, it is easy to spot the Cuthills winery by its burgundy metal roof. In the tasting room stands a cupboard filled with wine bottles dripping with shiny medals. The Swansons have won nearly one hundred medals in competition, though Ed Swanson waves them off casually as if they were trinkets from a carnival. The tasting room also holds jewelry designed and created by Holly Swanson, who began making jewelry in 1998. In addition to jewelry making, Holly helps out in the wine business and hosts wine-tastings all over Nebraska. The winery sponsors a Wine and Wings Blues Festival each August. The blues bands, food, and wine attract more than three thousand guests from all over the country. Years ago, Ed Swanson sang in a rock and roll band that toured the Midwest for ten years. Today, Nebraska's first contemporary vineyard provides inspiration and appreciation for the work of a modern-day pioneer.

APPENDIX

Vineyards and Wineries in South Dakota, Wyoming, and Nebraska

This list is complete as of January 2008.

Please contact the vineyards and wineries ahead of your visit to schedule an appointment or inquire about hours of operation and obtain directions.

South Dakota

Birdsong Vineyards: 30820 472d Ave., Beresford, SD 57004; telephone (605) 253-2132; web site: www.birdsongvineyards. com; e-mail: wine@birdsongvineyards.com. Contact: Phil or Donna Breed.

Black Hills Vineyard and Winery: 3339 E. Colorado Blvd., Spearfish, SD 57783; telephone (605) 664-9463; web site: www. blackhillswine.com; e-mail: thewinery@blackhillswine.com.

Chrisamari Estates Vineyard and Winery: 19141 Holly Rd., Pierre, SD 57501; telephone (605) 224-4778; web site: www. chrisamarivineyards.com; e-mail: admin@chrisamarivineyards. com. Contact: Randy Sarvis.

Dakota Falls Winery: 719 N. Splitrock Blvd., Brandon, SD 57005; telephone (605) 321-5532; e-mail: dakotafallswinery@sio.midco. net. Contact: Dave Howard.

Hahn Creek Winery: 47146 257th St., Crooks, SD 57020; telephone (605) 543-6995; web site: www.hahncreekwinery.com; e-mail: info@hahncreekwinery.com. Contact: Rich Hahn.

Jackson Winery and Vineyards: 1218 6th Ave., Belle Fourche, SD 57717.

Pete's Creek Winery: 912 Main St., Burke, SD 57523; telephone (605) 775-9060; e-mail: ahakin@sio.midco.net. Contact: Tim and Anita Hakin.

Prairie Berry Winery: 23837 Highway 385, Hill City, SD; telephone (605) 574-3898; web site: www.prairieberry.com; e-mail: mich@ prairieberry.com. Contact: Michele Slott.

Schadé Vineyard: 21095 463d Ave., Volga, SD 57071; telephone (605) 627-5545; web site: www.schadevineyard.com; e-mail: schade@itctel.com. Contact: Nancy Schadé.

Strawbale Winery: 47215 257th St., Renner, SD 57055; telephone (605) 543-5071; web site: www.strawbalewinery.com; e-mail: strawbalewine@alliancecom.net. Contact: Don or Susie South.

Syverson Vineyard: 21726 448th Ave., Oldham, SD 57051; telephone (605) 482-8385. Contact: Jim Syverson.

Valiant Vineyards: 1500 W. Main St., Vermillion, SD 57069; telephone (605) 624-4500; web site: www.valiantvineyards.com; e-mail: sherry@valiantvineyards.us. Contact: Sherry Nygaard.

Wide Sky Wines: 21091 1st Ave., Bushnell, SD 57276.

Wilde Prairie Winery: 48052 259th St., Brandon, SD 57005; telephone (605) 582-6471; web site: www.wildeprairiewinery.com;e-mail: wildeprairiewine@alliancecom.net. Contact: Jeff or Victoria Wilde.

Wyoming

Baker's Best Vineyard: 2866 Rd. 5, Chugwater, WY 82210.; telephone (307) 422-3502; e-mail: dwbaker@coffey.com. Contact: Teresa Baker.

Bass Farm Vineyard: 4954 Rd. 74, Torrington, WY 82240; telephone (307) 532-3944; e-mail: jbass@uwyo.edu. Contact: Del or Janet Bass.

Five Star Vineyards: 2396 Rd. 86, Lingle, WY 82223; telephone (307) 837-2237 or (307) 837-2023; e-mail: jandgbebo@scottsbluff.net or rosebebo@starband.net. Contact: Jolene or Rosie Bebo.

Hilltop Vineyard: 6 Hilltop Rd., Douglas, WY 82633; telephone (307) 358-9718 or (307) 358-2464; e-mail: hilltop_06@yahoo.com. Contact: Brad Johnson.

Irvin Cellar: 111 Webbwood Rd., Riverton, WY 82501; telephone (307) 856-2173; e-mail: rivertonirvincellar@msn.com. Contact: Kathleen Irvin.

LaGrange Vineyard: 1264 Rd. 51, LaGrange, WY 82221. Contact: Jim or Dianne Kallay.

Norman Farms Vineyard: Torrington, WY 82240; telephone (303) 697-3149; e-mail: bonhaase@comcast.net. Contact: Bonnie Haase.

North Hills Vineyard: Lingle, WY 82223; telephone (307) 837-2815. Contact: Dick Schutt.

Prairie Hills Vineyard: Cheyenne, WY

Prairie Justice Vineyard: P.O. Box 6, Chugwater, WY 82210; telephone (307) 422-3465; e-mail: johnjavaman@netzero.com. Contact: John Voight.

Rocky Ridge Vineyard: 1080 Vali Rd., Powell, WY 82435; telephone (307) 754-1051; e-mail: cpnapoli@tritel.net. Contact: Phil Napoli.

Sage Hill Vineyard: 1116 County Rd. 30 (P.O. Box 145), Chugwater, WY 82210; telephone (307) 422-3444; e-mail: sagehill@wyomail.com. Contact: Carol Eckhardt.

Spring Canyon Vineyard: 8675 Rd. 23, Lingle, WY 82223; telephone (307) 837-2545; e-mail: alkorell@scottsbluff.net. Contact: Alan or Terry Korell.

Swan Hill Vineyard: 1100 Slater Rd., Wheatland, WY 82201; telephone (307) 422-3305; e-mail: beauf@wyomail.com. Contact: Beauford Thompson.

Sybille Canyon Vineyard: 4681 Highway 34, Wheatland, WY 82201; e-mail: alternativechoices@yahoo.com. Contact: Sally Sanchez.

Table Mountain Vineyards: Box 24, Huntley, WY 82218; telephone (307) 459-0233; web site: www.tablemountainvineyards.com; e-mail: info@tablemountainvineyards.com. Contact: Patrick Zimmerer.

Wyoming Crafts and Wine Cellar: 331 Broadway, Sheridan, WY 82801; telephone (307) 673-0291; e-mail: wine@fiberpipe.net. Contact: Deena John.

Nebraska

Aspire Cellars: 1402 Dennis Dean Rd., Ashland, NE 68003; telephone (402) 203-1722; web site: www.aspirecellars.com; e-mail: aspirecellars@cox.net. Contact: Richard Hilske.

Big Cottonwood Vineyards and Winery: 2865 County Rd. I, Tekamah, NE 68061; telephone (402) 374-2656; web site: www. bigcottonwood.com; e-mail: bigcottonwood@huntel.net. Contact: Deb Barnett.

Bohemian Alps Vineyard: 2751 X Rd., Brainard, NE 68626; telephone (402) 545-3871; e-mail: janbostelman@dtnspeed.net. Contact: Bruce or Jan Bostelman.

Calf Creek Vineyards: 35181 Calf Creek Rd., Mullen, NE 69152; telephone (308) 546-2853; e-mail: ccvineyards@neb-sandhills. net. Contact: Deb Cox.

Cedar Hills Vineyard-Gardens and Tasting Room: 48970 375th Rd., Ravenna, NE 68869; telephone (308) 452-3181; web site: www.cedarhillsvineyard.com; e-mail: japsears@rcom-ne.com. Contact: Paul or Joyce Sears.

Cuthills Vineyards: 54663 853 Rd., Pierce, NE 68767; telephone (402) 329-6774; web site: www.cuthills.com; e-mail: visitus@cuthills. com. Contact: Ed or Holly Swanson.

Deer Springs Winery: 16255 Adams St., Lincoln, NE 68527; telephone (402) 327-8738; web site: www.deerspringswinery.com; e-mail: info@deerspringswinery.com. Contact: Jennifer Reeder.

Echo Hill Vineyard: 710 White Feathers Ct., Arlington, NE 68002; telephone (402) 478-4538; e-mail: mmullins@huntel.com. Contact: Rich Mullins.

Fagowi Vineyard: 3700 Ash Rd., St. Edward, NE 68660; telephone (402) 678-3399. Contact: Frank Jasa.

Feather River Vineyards: 6152 SE State Farm Rd., North Platte, NE 69101; telephone (308) 530-5744; web site: www.feather-river. com. Contact: Connie Brittan.

Five Star Vineyard: 520 Eldora, Lincoln, NE 68505; web site: www. vintagenebraska.org; e-mail: fivestarvineyard@aol.com. Contact: John Fischbach.

Four Winds Vineyard: 1033 County Rd. 5, Ashland, NE 68003; telephone (402) 944-9463; web site: www.fwvwines.com; e-mail: vinesandwines@hotmail.com. Contact: Teresa Kresak.

Foxhill Vineyards: 800 N. Seventeenth St., Tekamah, NE 68061; telephone (402) 374-1484; e-mail: foxhill@huntel.net. Contact: Al or Connie Faltys.

Harmony Vineyards: 801 Candice St., Valentine, NE 69201; telephone (402) 376-3739; e-mail: harmony@shwisp.net. Contact: Ron or Sandy Billings.

HRB Vineyard: 3074 County Rd. I, Weston, NE 68070; telephone (402) 642-0900; e-mail: heather@clarks.net. Contact: Heather Byers.

Ida's Vitis Vineyard: Roscoe, NE 69153; telephone (308) 284-6699; e-mail: kjgamet@charter.net. Contact: John Gamet.

James Arthur Vineyards: 2001 W. Raymond Rd., Raymond, NE 68428; telephone (402) 783-5255; web site: www.jamesarthurvineyards.com; e-mail: wines@cornhusker.net. Contact: Jim Ballard.

Johann Jakob Link Vineyard: 51375 310th Rd., Ravenna, NE 68869; telephone (308) 467-2322. Contact: Dale Link.

Kimmel Orchard and Vineyard: 5995 G Rd., Nebraska City, NE 68410; telephone (402) 873-5293; web site: www.kimmelorchard.com; e-mail: eolson@arbordayfarm.org. Contact: Erik Olson.

Last Chance Winery tasting rooms: 114 NE First St., Mullen, NE 69152; telephone (308) 546-2960; and 48970 375th Rd., Ravenna, NE 68869; telephone (308) 546-2960. Contact: Deb Cox.

Lincoln Highway Vineyard: 10320 Willow Rd., Shelton, NE 68876; telephone (402) 894-0515. Contact: Glenn Schanou.

Lovers Lane Vineyard: 815 Lovers Ln., Columbus, NE 68601; telephone (402) 563-2295; e-mail: llvineyard@neb.rr.com. Contact: Frank Loomer.

Mac's Creek Vineyards and Winery: 43315 Rd. 757, Lexington, NE 68850; telephone/fax (308) 324-0440; web site: www.macscreekvineyards.com; e-mail: barry@macscreekvineyards.com. Contact: Max McFarland.

Millenium Wines: 75137 Highway 283, Lexington, NE 68850; telephone (308) 324-6094; open by appointment only.

Miretta Vineyards and Winery: 1732 Highway 281, St. Paul, NE 68873; telephone (308) 754-5567; web site: www.mirettavineyards.com; e-mail: lorettamcdowell@charter.net. Contact: Mick or Loretta McDowell.

Nissen Winery: 88560 566th Ave., Hartington, NE 68739; telephone (402) 254-3426; web site: www.nissenwine.com; e-mail: tnissen@hartel.net. Contact: Tim or David Nissen.

Pheasant Oak Vineyard Confections: 2231 32d Rd., Brainard, NE 68626; telephone (402) 545-2078; web site: www.pheasantoak. com.

Ponderosa Vineyards: 11753 710 Rd., Alma, NE 68920; telephone (308) 928-2291; e-mail: adneapp@cenebr.net. Contact: Harold Smolik.

Prairie Creek Vineyards: 2321 Thirteenth Rd., Central City, NE 68826; telephone (308) 940-1370; web site: www.prairiecreekwine. com; e-mail: prairiecreekwine@gmail.com. Contact: Nicholas Ryan.

Prairie Knolls Vineyard: 620 Eighth Ave., St. Paul, NE 68873; telephone (308) 687-6872; e-mail: annmrief@yahoo.com. Contact: Ann Rief.

Prairie Star Vineyard: 475 Sprague Rd., Roca, NE 68430; telephone (402) 794-9104; e-mail: kbbatie@windstream.net. Contact: Kim or Barb Batie.

Prairie View Vineyard: 1333 Prairie View Rd., Eagle, NE 68347; telephone (402) 310-9338; e-mail: barth@unlserve.unl.edu. Contact: Bart Holmquist.

Prairie Vine Vineyard and Winery: 1463 Seventeenth Ave., Mitchell, NE 69357; telephone (308) 623-2955; web site: www.prairievine. com; e-mail: allen@prairievine.com. Contact: Allen or Carlene Gall.

Prairie Wings Vineyard: 6659 Otoe Rd., Alliance, NE 69301; telephone (308) 762-3051; e-mail: giles98@telecomwest.net. Contact: Gene or Jane Giles.

Prairyerth Vineyard: 2803 E. Union Rd., Union, NE 68455; telephone (402) 558-8524; web site: www.arbortrailswinery.com; e-mail: muelleman@cox.net. Contact: Bob Muelleman.

Prime Country Winery: 12120 Southwest 142d St., Denton, NE 68339; telephone (402) 826-3567; web site: www.primecountrywinery. com; e-mail OG35349@alltel.net. Contact: Orville Gertsch.

Ravenswood Road Vineyard: 71497 Ravenswood Rd., McCook, NE 69001; telephone (308) 345-6176. Contact: Harold Davidson.

Reno Ridge Vineyard: 75351 Rd. 425, Cozad, NE 69130; telephone
(308) 324-5138. Contact: Kim Rhone.

Rosehill Winery: 305 Seminary St., Stromsburg, NE 68666;
telephone (402) 764-7391; e-mail: koinzan@alltel.net. Contact:
Dennis Koinzan.

Sage Hill Vineyards and Winery: 32621 Rock Creek Rd., Parks,
NE 69041; telephone (308) 423-2062; web site: www.
sagehillvineyards.com; e-mail: walkers@bwtelcom.net. Contact:
Hal or Carol Walker.

SchillingBridge Winery and Microbrewery: 62193 710th Rd.,
Pawnee City, NE 68420; telephone (402) 852-2400; web
site: www.schillingbridgewinery.com; e-mail: sharon@
schillingbridgewinery.com. Contact: Sharon or Mike Schilling.

17 Ranch Winery: 304 Main St., Lewellen, NE 69147; telephone (308)
778-5542; web site: agonline.com/17Ranch; e-mail: 17ranch@
scottsbluff.net. Contact: Ellen Burdick.

Silvercreek Hill Vineyards and Winery: 3130 County Rd. M,
Tekamah, NE 68061; telephone (402) 870-0083 or (402)
870-0084; web site: www.silvercreekhill.com; e-mail:
silvercreekhill@yahoo.com. Contact: June or Phil Simpson.

Slattery Vintage Estates: 8925 Adams St., Nehawka, NE 68413;
telephone (402) 267-5267; e-mail: ems@reinschslattery.com.
Contact: Mike or Barb Slattery.

Soaring Wings Vineyard: 17111 S. 138th St., Springfield, NE 68059;
telephone (402) 253-2479; web site: www.soaringwingswine.
com; e-mail: info@soaringwingswine.com. Contact: Sharon
Shaw.

South Fork Vineyard: 845 Rd. East D, Ogallala, NE 69153; telephone
(308) 284-6394; web site: www.southforkvineyard.com; e-mail:
southfrk@megavision.com. Contact: Jackie Hopken.

Superior Estates Winery: 200 W. 15th St., Superior, NE
68978; telephone (402) 391-1823 or (402) 879-3001; web
site: www.superiorestateswinery.com; e-mail: info@
superiorestateswinery.com. Contact: Randy or Kelly Meyer.

Three Brothers Vineyard and Winery: 812 Lincoln, Farnham, NE
69029; telephone (308) 569-2501; e-mail: glwach@atcjet.net.
Contact: Gary or Ricky Sue Wach.

Vybiral Vineyard: 1311 County Rd. 13, Wahoo, NE 68066; telephone
(402) 366-1546; e-mail: ajvybiral@yahoo.com. Contact: Al
Vybiral.

Wehling Vineyards: 80045 Rd. 429, Broken Bow, NE 68822;
telephone (308) 872-5583; e-mail: edandmaxine@hotmail.com.
Contact: Ed or Maxine Wehling.

Whiskey Run Creek Vineyard and Winery: 702 Main St.,
Brownville, NE 68321; telephone (402) 825-4601; web site: www.
whiskeyruncreek.com; e-mail: whiskeyrun@alltel.net. Contact:
Ron Heskett.

Whispering Vines Winery: 3110 W. Branched Oak Rd., Raymond, NE
68428; telephone (402) 783-2875; e-mail: djlilyhorn@inebraska.
com. Contact: Dale Lilyhorn.

Wigle Creek Vineyard: Homer, NE 68030; telephone (402) 698-2421.
Contact: Kent Rasmussen.

Wynkoop Vineyard: 1624 S. Ninth St., Nebraska City, NE 68410;
telephone (402) 873-4701; e-mail: wynrol@wmconnect.com.
Contact: Ron or Shari Wynkoop

GLOSSARY

Aging—storing wine to allow it to mature

Basket press—a traditional wine press with a wooden basket and a ratchet system used to extract juice or wine from must

Bladder press—a wine press with an internal rubber bladder that expands to press must against the sides of the outer cage in order to extract juice or wine

Blending—mixing two or more wines together to adjust the flavor, acid, or aromas of the finished product

Bouquet—the scent a wine develops, adding to its character

Bud—a compressed dormant shoot at the base of each leaf stem on a grapevine that begins growing in the spring

Bud break—the initial growth of buds in the spring

Cane—a grapevine shoot that has turned brown and woody

Canopy—the canes, shoots, and leaves of a grapevine

Carboy—a large bottle sometimes used in winemaking

Compost—partially rotted vegetable matter used as fertilizer

Cordon—the permanent wood on a grapevine, also called an arm

Crushing—mashing fresh grapes into a pulp

Enology—the science of winemaking

Fermentation—the process that converts sugar into alcohol, changing grape juice into wine

Fertilizing—adding plant nutrients to the soil

Filtering—removing sediments or yeast from wine

Fining—adding a substance to wine to remove cloudiness

Foxy finish—a sharp bite in the flavor of a wine

Fruity or fruit forward—a dominant fruitiness in the flavor of a wine

Graft—to splice together two different grape woods

Grow tubes—cylinders placed around newly planted grapevines to provide protection and promote growth

Malolactic fermentation—the process of changing malic acid to lactic acid, often by introducing bacteria into fermenting wine, in order to soften a wine's taste

Must—a mixture of crushed grapes, juice, stems, and skins

Oaking—aging wine in oak barrels or soaking oak chips in wine to add flavor

pH—a measure of acidity

Pressing—squeezing juice or wine from a must with a grape press

Primary fermentation—the initial step in winemaking, when yeast converts about two-thirds of the sugar in a must to alcohol

Pruning—cutting off any portion of a grapevine to control vine size, vigor, or crop production

Punching down—mixing the risen skin and pulp on a must back down into the juice during primary fermentation

Racking—siphoning wine from one container to another to separate the wine from any sediment

Secondary fermentation—the process of turning any sugar left after primary fermentation into alcohol

Shoot—the growing structure that emerges from buds

Stemmer-crusher—a machine that removes stems from clusters of grapes and crushes the grapes to form a must

Tannin—a bitter substance contained primarily in grape stems

Training—tying and pruning vines to achieve a desired arrangement on a trellis

Trellis—a support system for grapevines that maximizes the amount of sunlight vines receive

Two-wire trellis—the most common type of trellis, consisting of two horizontal wires spaced about a foot apart and strung between vertical posts

Three-wire trellis—a trellis with three horizontal wires strung between vertical posts, giving the grower extra places to tie vines

Vertical-shoot-position trellis—a trellis with guide wires to arrange shoots and thereby control the growth of the canopy

Viticulture—the science of growing grapes

Yeast—one-celled plants that convert sugar to alcohol and change grape juice into wine

SELECTED BIBLIOGRAPHY

Blosser, Susan Sokol. *At Home in the Vineyard: Cultivating a Winery, an Industry, and a Life*. Berkeley: University of California Press, 2006.

Cox, Jeff. *From Vines to Wines: The Complete Guide to Growing Grapes and Making Your Own Wine*. North Adams, Mass.: Storey Publishing, 1999.

Hargrave, Louisa Thomas. *The Vineyard: A Memoir*. New York: Penguin Books, 2003.

Jackson, David, and Danny Schuster. *The Production of Grapes & Wines in Cool Climates*. Aoteroa, New Zealand: Gypsum Press, 2001.

Kooser, Ted. *Local Wonders: Seasons in the Bohemian Alps*. Lincoln: University of Nebraska Press, 2002.

Krosch, Penelope, comp. *With a Tweezers in One Hand and a Book in the Other: The Grape Breeding Work of Elmer Swenson*. N.p.: By the Compiler, 2005.

Macgregor, David. *Growing Grapes in Minnesota*. N.p.: Minnesota Grape Growers Association, [1977].

McGrew, John R., Juergen Loenholdt, Thomas J. Zabadal, Arthur C. Hunt, and Herman O. Amberg. *Growing Wine Grapes*. Ann Arbor, Mich.: G. W. Kent, 1993.

Nixon, Lance. "Grape Growers Have Language of Their Own: Foxy. Earthy. Valiant." *Farm and Home Research* 52 (2001): 13–19.

Ode, David J. *Dakota Flora: A Seasonal Sampler*. Pierre: South Dakota State Historical Society Press, 2006.

Plocher, Thomas, and Robert J. Parke. *Northern Winework: Growing Grapes and Making Wine in Cold Climates*. Hugo, Minn.: Northern Winework, 2001.

Rombough, Lon. *The Grape Grower: A Guide to Organic Viticulture*. White River Junction, Vt.: Chelsea Green Publishing, 2002.

Smart, Richard, and Mike Robinson. *Sunlight into Wine: A Handbook for Winegrape Canopy Management*. Adelaide, Australia: Winetitles, 1991.

Waggener, Robert. "Taste of Success." *UWyo: The Magazine for Alumni and Friends of the University of Wyoming* 5 (2004): 12–15.

Winkler, A. J., J. A. Cook, W. M. Kliewer, and L. A. Lider. *General Viticulture*. Berkeley: University of California Press, 1974.

INDEX

Numbers in **bold** indicate photographs